CONTEMPORARY APPROACHES to COGNITION

CONTEMPORARY APPROACHES

to COGNITION

A Symposium Held at the University of Colorado

Contributors

Jerome S. Bruner
Egon Brunswik
Leon Festinger
Fritz Heider
Karl F. Muenzinger
Charles E. Osgood
David Rapaport

HARVARD UNIVERSITY PRESS · CAMBRIDGE

Distributed in Great Britain by
Oxford University Press, London

Third Printing, 1968

Library of Congress Catalogue Card Number: 57–12963

Printed in the United States of America

FOREWORD

This book undoubtedly reflects the *Zeitgeist*, but our major aim is to influence it. For a long time psychology in America has slighted what may be considered to be its ultimate purpose, the scientific understanding of man's cognitive behavior. The reasons for ignoring cognitive phenomena have been manifold, but prominent among them were the difficulties in achieving the degree of rigor and objectivity demanded by a self-consciously scientific psychology. Such standards could be met only if one stayed very close to observable events, stimuli, and responses, and to proximal rather than distal ones. Recent years, however, have loosened the hold of narrow operationism, and psychologists have felt free, as well as stimulated, to attack perhaps less precise but certainly far more interesting and significant problems of human behavior. This is the *Zeitgeist* that motivated us to arrange a symposium on the topic of cognition.

It was our intention to organize the contributions of the participants around a unified plan. The first paper presents a historical introduction to the topic of cognition as well as the author's own orientation and recent research. The next four papers represent particular viewpoints in psychology, summarizing conceptual problems and empirical findings. The final contributor undertook the task of providing a synopsis of the symposium as well as future trends in cognition.

The names and the work of the participants are too well known to psychologists to require further introduction. The orientations of the papers in this volume range from behaviorism to psychoanalysis to information theory, and in them is reported experimental work that has not been available heretofore. The Symposium was held on the University of Colorado campus May 12–14, 1955, with all participants excepting the late Egon Brunswik present throughout. The subsequent death of Professor Brunswik was a major loss for psychology, and especially for the area of cognition.

Beyond the quality and scope of the formal papers, the meetings were enlivened by the stimulating and provocative criticisms and interchanges among the participants after each paper. Unfortunately, only a portion of these could be included in this volume.

On behalf of the Psychology Department of the University of Colorado the undersigned committee assumed the responsibility of planning the Symposium. The Department wishes to extend special thanks to Vice President W. F. Dyde for his efforts in obtaining the generous financial support that the University provided.

If this book helps to develop further theoretical and empirical work relating to the problem of cognition it will have satisfied both its contributors and its sponsors.

The Cognition Symposium Committee
Howard E. Gruber
Kenneth R. Hammond
Richard Jessor

CONTENTS

CONTEMPORARY APPROACHES
to COGNITION

INTRODUCTION

Karl F. Muenzinger

Professor of Psychology, Emeritus, *University of Colorado*

IT IS with deep satisfaction that I welcome the opening of the Symposium on Cognition. Symposia on special areas in psychology, such as motivation, emotion, learning, cerebral mechanisms, and others, have become rather frequent lately, and for a good reason. The annual meetings of the American Psychological Association have grown so large in the last twenty-five years that it has become less and less profitable — at least professionally — to attend them and exchange with one's colleagues ideas and experiences in research activities. This is a serious loss, which has been counteracted in various ways, among which the arrangement of symposia is one of the best. They permit concentration on a single topic, which is treated by several experts through different approaches, while also providing participation by the audience through discussion. The frustration of having to choose between parallel meetings is absent as are the personal distractions, pleasant though they might be. As far as I am aware, the present Symposium is the first one in the field of psychology to concern itself with the important and difficult area of cognition.

I have been asked to make a few comments by way of a preface, on a topic of my own choosing. In doing so I shall leave the area of cognition to our distinguished guest writers. Instead, I would like to say a few words about a subject that is related to cognition only in a very general way, namely, the subject of *the identifiability of the referent in psychology*.

In physics, chemistry, and other physical sciences there is as a rule no difficulty with the meanings of technical terms. Once a term has been chosen to refer to a certain object or process, the discourse proceeds without any danger that the author and the listener or reader may be at variance with respect to the referent. Neither can it happen that the author shifts, without being aware of it, the referents of his terms as he goes along, talking about one object or process at one time and a slightly different one at other times, while still using the same term. We may say that physicists communicate about things and what these things do, and need not — and ordinarily do not — argue about their terms.

The ideal situation exists in mathematics, where arbitrary symbols are assigned to the major referents at the beginning of the discussion, and the relation between referent and symbol is strictly adhered to until the end. The symbols for the operations are usually the conventional ones, but if one wishes to change an operation even slightly, a new symbol is used or the variation is explicitly stated. The discussion is about the referents and not about the symbols and what referents one might or should assign to them. The referents are identified unambiguously.

It is in psychology that the identifiability of the referent is a major difficulty, a difficulty that besets the use of common terms. A number of years ago there was published a series of articles by various authors on the question of "What is Learning?" From the point of view taken here, this was a concerted attempt to "discover," if you please, the referent of the word "learning." The series was not concerned with the nature of the various referents that were suggested, but essentially with the usage of a term!

When described in this way, does not this series seem to be a waste of good journal space which is not only unjustifiable but also rather naïve? Why, I asked myself, did these authors not see that in order to advance their science and specialty they should have reversed the question and asked, after identifying the processes with which they were concerned, what is a serviceable term for a particular practice?

Psychology abounds in such sterile exercises. Let me remind you of the literature on similar "what is" discussions. What is an instinct, what is an emotion, or what is apperception? If some of these questions were asked too long ago for you to remember them clearly, let me remind you of a notable instance that occurred more recently: namely, the confusion caused by the diversity of the referents of the term "rigidity." The "what is" questions are a symptom of a major difficulty in our field, a manifestation of a linguistic immaturity that will, I trust, be overcome eventually.

The result of this difficulty is impaired communication. Not only is there a danger that a term may have one referent as used by one worker in the field and a different referent as used by another worker, there is also the danger that a referent may change in chameleonlike fashion within a single discussion by the same author. Consider the term "stimulus." At first an author may restrict himself to the referent coupled with this term as "the energy of sound or light, and so on, affecting a receptor," but finally the referent may be identified, after many slight additions and changes, as an entire social situation. The result of such scientific punning is that the unwarranted and unproven assumption is slipped into the discourse, an assumption which may not be perceived by the unwary reader, that the properties of the original referent can be transferred legitimately to the last referent. But actually we may be dealing here with a series of referents, each of which differs slightly from its neighbors, while the first and last members of the series are so far apart that there is little overlapping between them.

The only and obvious way of minimizing this difficulty of shifted referents is to identify the referent first and then name the term with which it will be coupled for the time being.

The result would be that a discussion would be concerned with referents, as it should be, and not with terminology, which should occupy only a minimal space. Another result might be the elimination of what a colleague of ours has called "rubberband theories," which are conveniently stretched in order to meet any objection or criticism. Eventually we might also teach our students that verbal identity does not make referents identical, and illustrate this dictum with the case history of the term "rigidity."

SCOPE AND ASPECTS
OF THE COGNITIVE PROBLEM

Egon Brunswik

University of California

ONE of the broadest and most universally accepted definitions of psychology conceives of psychology as being concerned with the interrelationships between organism and environment. In this definition both organism and environment appear as equal partners. This is not to say that they must be equal in all aspects of structural detail. We know that this would mean carrying things too far. A better simile would be to compare the two partners with a married couple. Perhaps the organism could be seen as playing the role of the husband and the environment that of the wife, or the reverse may be argued as well.

At any rate, both organism and environment will have to be seen as systems, each with properties of its own, yet both hewn from basically the same block. Each has surface and depth, or overt and covert regions. As in any marriage, the interrelationship between the two systems has the essential characteristic of a "coming-to-terms." And this coming-to-terms is not merely a matter of the mutual boundary or surface areas. It concerns equally as much, or perhaps even more, the rapport between the central, covert layers of the two systems. It follows that, much as psychology must be concerned with the texture of the organism or of its nervous processes and must investigate them in depth, it also must be concerned with the texture of the environment as it extends in depth away from the common boundary.

It will have been noted that by environment we mean the measurable characteristics of the objective surroundings of the organism rather than the psychological environment or life space, in the sense in which Lewin has used this term. We may specify the sum total of these objective surroundings as the "ecology" of an individual or species.

It is the contention of this paper that if there is anything that still ails psychology in general, and the psychology of cognition specifically, it is the neglect of investigation of environmental or ecological texture in favor of that of the texture of organismic structures and processes. Both historically and systematically psychology has forgotten that it is a science of organism–environment relationships, and has become a science of the organism. No such drastic statement can be literally true, of course. Defenders of the traditional policies of psychology will point to the fact that almost anywhere in modern psychology the organism is seen as in contact and interaction with the environment, be this in the form of "input" or "output" or both. But my point is that the investigation is in the typical case not carried beyond these boundary points into the territory of the environment proper, while on the other hand it is richly engrossed in the organismic portions of the causal chains, those portions that connect input with output on the "inside." This preoccupation of the psychologist with the organism at the expense of the environment is somewhat reminiscent of the position taken by those inflatedly masculine medieval theologians who granted a soul to men but denied it to women; our point, then, is to restore or establish the proper equality of standards in the treatment of organism and environment — that is, the equality of subject and situation (or object) in which equal justice is done to the inherent characteristics of the organism and of the environment.

Cognitive Achievement, Strategy, Tactics

But let me be more specific. Let me concentrate on the problem of cognition, which we may define as the problem of the acquisition of knowledge. Within cognition, let me concentrate on the more general case, on the more intuitive type of cognition called perception. And let me assume that this special form of cognition may serve as a paradigm of the patterns prevailing elsewhere in behavior. Within perception, let me choose topics sufficiently complex so as to encompass cognitive patterns in all their potential ramifications. To make reasonably sure that this is the case, we should sample cognitive problems representatively much as, in the study of personality, we sample persons and then survey the full sample of problems as to their structural components. But perhaps we can substitute for this rather forbidding ideal a choice of problems of such a degree of spread and intricacy that it is very likely that none of the major aspects or phases of the cognitive problem will be left unrepresented.

The problems I propose to choose are those of three-dimensional perception of space and of the "things" in it, and of the physiognomic or social perception of personality traits from external appearance. Both of these groups of problems have been with us for a long time, and offer the possibility of studying historical climates as they may affect the approach to a certain problem. Both have been highly puzzling in a variety of ways, and have revealed a great many facets as the context of the problem was varied.

This richness, in turn, must be seen as the result of the fact that both groups of problems fulfill the requirement with which we have begun our considerations. Both of them do not halt at the boundary between organism and environment but penetrate into the very heart of the environment. If the respective cognitive achievements approach perfection, the type of object attained is a remote one, or, more precisely, one defined without reference to the particular retinal input elicited by it in a given situation. Using a pair of terms first suggested by Koffka (18) and by Heider (13), both thing-perception and social perception involve cognitive attainment of "distal" variables that are to a certain extent independently variable of the corresponding "proximal" or sensory input. The measured size of a physical body and the tested intelligence of a person are examples of distal variables, while the size of the retinal impact and the geometric relations in the face or photograph of the person whose intelligence is to be intuitively appraised are examples of relatively proximal variables.

The distinction between distal and proximal concerns the measured properties of the environment only, taking the chains of event to a point just prior to their impact on the organism. The first impact upon the organism, or the relatively outlying portions of the excitatory processes or mechanism, are usually called "peripheral." And the final stage of the cognitive process is "central." We need not be concerned here with the fact that the central event must in turn be encoded in verbalized judgment to become communicable and conveniently measurable.

The full scope of the cognitive problem, at least so far as external perception is concerned, would then seem to involve a theater stretching all the way from the distal to the central layers. Its prime aspect would seem to be the over-all correspondence between a certain distal and a certain central variable, so that the former could be considered successfully mapped into the latter. This first aspect we call cognitive "achievement" or "attainment," or also "functional validity" of the final response relative to the distal focus.

The second aspect of the cognitive problem concerns the gross characteristics or macrostructure of the pattern of proximal and peripheral mediation between the distal and central foci. This is the problem of the grand strategy of mediation. Of special importance in this context is the question of whether or not a single track of mediation is sufficient or whether a multiplicity of cues or mechanisms must be provided. It is here that the necessity of special inquiry into the texture of the environment per se becomes evident for the first time. Obviously, a single track of mediation can be sufficient only if the environment provides us with unequivocal proximal or peripheral indicators or cues. For example, if Aristotle had been right in his assumption that all those whose faces resemble that of a fox are sly, and if this should be true in reverse also, the single cue of foxlike appearance would be sufficient cognitively to attain slyness in others. But we suspect that such does not hold — as indeed such ideal relationships do not in the general case — and that therefore macromediation must use alternative pathways. In other words, it is subject to the same principle of "vicarious functioning," which since Hunter's presidential address in 1932 must be recognized as the basic definiens of all behavior.

A third aspect of the cognitive problem is given by the attempt to break down the cognitive process further into its component parts. It concerns the special technology of the machinery along each of the several possible tracks of mediation. It may therefore be labeled the problem of micromediation, or of mediational tactics. The special ways in which foxlike appearance, if any, may be established neurologically furnish an example of such a problem.

Ecological and Organismic Phase of the Cognitive Process

The threefold distinction among the achievement, the strategy, and the tactics of the cognitive process concerns the order of magnitude of the unit encompassed. Achievement and its strategy are molar problems; tactics is a molecular problem. There is a second way of subdividing the cognitive process, one that proceeds in terms of regional segmentation. Here the most obvious distinction is obtained by breaking up the over-all achievement arc into an ecological and an organismic portion. The final distal–central correspondences may then be analyzed in terms of (a) distal–proximal correspondences, which are intraecological; (b) proximal–peripheral correspondences, which cross over the boundary from the environment into the organism; and (c) peripheral–central correspondences, which are intraorganismic. For most of the molar problems of cognition the distinction between the proximal and peripheral layers is of lesser importance, however, and only the first and third of our correspondence problems remain in prominence today.

We had already encountered the purely ecological portion of the cognitive process when we spoke of the possibility of its equivocality and of the ensuing necessity facing the organism of having to compensate for this equivocality by the use of additional or "vicarious" cues. The degree of distal–proximal correspondence involved here may be labeled "ecological validity." Just as the functional validity or correctness of judgment may be expressed by a correlation coefficient linking the central response variable with the distal variable, ecological validities may be expressed by correlations linking the proximal with the distal variable. Turning to our example from Aristotle, the over-all functional validity of judgments of slyness would be given by the degree of the statistical association of these judgments with tested slyness in the object. The ecological validity, on the other hand, would not involve the final judgment. It would merely be an expression of the degree of statistical association between tested slyness in the object and one of the potential mediators of this objective slyness to the perceiver: in our case, foxlike features. So long as we confine our attention to ecological validities we are therefore dealing with a sign–significate relationship in its capacity as a challenge to the cognitive powers of the perceiver, but we do not yet know whether or not the perceiver will be responsive to the cue. Since in the typical case these sign–significate relationships will be far from univocal and the ecological validity will therefore be far from perfect, some may even doubt whether the responding organism would be justified in using the proximal cue as a basis for judgment regarding the distal object.

Be this as it may, our next concern must be this second, intraorganismic portion of the cognitive process. We shall speak of this as the phase of the "utilization" of cues. Those who take the position that all of psychology must deal with the organism per se, rather than also spreading out into the environment, may wish to confine the term "cognitive process" to this second phase. We would prefer to do otherwise and consider utilization as something like the third act of a play, one that culminates and resolves an earlier setting or impasse and that cannot be understood without such external build-up. The third act is the crux of a play. There are good third acts and there are poor or weak ones, depending on how the potential of the build-up is realized. Similarly, in cognition, the utilization of the sensory input relative to the distal object may be appropriate or not. We may call it appropriate in a generalized sense if the strength of utilization of a cue is in line with the degree of its ecological validity; but we must remember that individual cognitive failure is compatible with such general appropriateness in all instances running counter to the prevalent trend of ecological validity.

Prescientific Approach to Cognition. Cognitive Absolutism

Let me now turn to the unfolding of the drama of cognition before the eyes of the curious onlooker. Let me distinguish two types of such onlookers. One is exemplified by the philosophers, including those casual scientists in whose minds incidental observation, practical problems, and abstract speculation are found in curious mixture. The other is the scientist proper. The latter type of onlooker supersedes the former in the course of history, although there is a great deal of overlapping.

Let us see how the two types of approach have gone about handling the cognitive problem. First, the philosophers have tended to proceed primarily at the most global level. In our own somewhat disenchanting terminology this means concentration on the achievement problem at the expense of those of the strategy and tactics of mediation. Kant's formulation as to whether the "thing in itself" is knowable is perhaps the penultimate in a long chain of different phrasings of the problem of achievement as they spring from the original blandness of naïve realism.

A second feature of the philosophical approach to cognition is its tendency toward absolute, all-or-none solutions of the achievement problem. In naïve realism, at least in its most extreme form, perfect functional validity is taken for granted in such a manner that stimulus and response, or reality and appearance, become in effect one and the same. But soon the pendulum swings to the opposite extreme, skepticism. Once the possibility of error is discovered, there seem to be at first no bounds to the generalization of error. Skepticism thus has been said to proceed by the assumption "once a liar, always a liar." But it was a great skeptic, Democritus, who, by the good services of his observations on perceptual error, came to assign independent status to the stimulus, and indeed to define it in essentially quantitative, mensurational terms. Because he opened the door to the operational approach to the problem of cognition, we may agree with those who rank Democritus on a par with the two acknowledged great men of ancient philosophy, Plato and Aristotle. It is only by an operational approach that we may discover that cognition may be sometimes right and sometimes wrong, and that therefore our treatment of the cognitive problem must be probabilistic. As we will see, cognitive absolutism is still rampant in modern perception psychology, and it appears in a variety of rather treacherous disguises.

The fact that philosophers tended to concentrate on the achievement aspect by no means blinded them to the demands of the mediation problem. But in entering this area they did so predominantly in their secondary capacity as amateur scientists, and sometimes the mechanics of practical aspects became altogether dominant. Physiognomic perception has always been a ball tossed among philosophy, medicine, and the country fair. And the first to list the depth cues by which the painter could restore the three-dimensionality of his original to his picture was a great artist and engineer, Leonardo da Vinci. Philosophers took over promptly from there, with Descartes and Berkeley in the forefront of those who helped to round out our knowledge of the strategy of three-dimensional perception.

Classification of Cues in Terms of Peripheral Tactics

This was about the state of affairs when psychology began to emerge in its own right about a century ago, and thus the problem of cognition became capable of scientific treatment. The over-all skeleton of the problem was there, even though the traditional metaphysical formulations all but hid the fact that the achievement problem was scientifically meaningful; there was some scattered attention to mediational strategy, but practically nothing was filled in regarding mediational tactics.

Two major alternatives seem open at this point: either science could retrace the process of analysis from top to bottom or it could take a reverse course and begin with tactics. The latter is what actually happened. At first glance this proposition seems to be begging the question. How could one study tactics if one did not have a clear picture of the context of these tactics? But we must remember that in a vague and at the same time somewhat absolute way the problem of cognition had been posed with some measure of success in philosophy, and that this anticipatory treatment was sufficient to furnish some kind of informal matrix for the problems of tactics to hold on to.

Tactics is, as we have seen, a form of elementism, and one of the first things we all have learned in history is that nineteenth-century psychology was elementistic. The point we wish to stress in the present context is that the elementism of the "punctiform sensations reunited by the bond of association," which usually serves as the prime paradigm for elementism, is but one of many manifestations within a much richer syndrome. The type of elementism which we should like to expose by the rather crude summary statement that, in psychological science, the study of cognition tends to begin with the study of cognitive tactics has little to do with the introspective sensationism of the period. Rather, it lays stress on the objective processes involved in cognition.

Problems of tactics are characterized by (a) concentration on a single track of mediation, (b) encapsulation within the organismic portion of this cognitive track, (c) occupation with tracing this track step by step, and thus (d) concentration on the peripheral physiological phase, that phase which constitutes the beginning of the intraorganismic leg of the cognitive process.

An example is furnished by the traditional modes of classification of the so-called perceptual depth criteria. As we have hinted above, the difficulties of appraising depth on the basis of two-dimensional retinal projection had been sufficiently real-

ized during the philosophical era, and it had been acknowledged that utilization of a variety of such cues was an essential
strategic requirement. Lists of such cues were thus inherited
from an earlier phase of history, but their classification had
yet to be undertaken. Three major traditional classificatory
schemes may be distinguished. They all reveal concentration
of attention on the tactics of the organism.

The first of the traditional tactical classifications is that into
primary versus secondary cues. There are only three primary
cues: binocular disparity, binocular convergence, and accommodation. Closer inspection shows that in each case there is
a gross peripheral organ or mechanism with which the functioning of the cue may be identified. In the case of binocular
disparity this is the presence of a neurologically integrated
double eye with the optic chiasma and the respective centers.
In the case of convergence there are the extrinsic muscles controlling the rotation of the eyeball. And in the case of accommodation there is the ciliary muscle controlling the curvature
of the lens. None of the other depth criteria can boast such
obvious peripheral machinery. Thus we find them relegated
to a "secondary" role, like paupers without a house or a car
of their own. Their utilization potential is also seen as marred;
only the primary cues are said to be capable of furnishing genuine experiences of depth, the secondary cues leading at best
to pale surrogates without genuine plasticity.

The presence of a striking peripheral physiological mechanism turns out to be a status symbol of even greater consequences. It is the existence of primary cues that lends some
of the major support to the doctrine of nativism regarding
space, much as if such more centrally determined principles
as the autochthonous dynamics of the brain field which the
Gestaltists have later brought into the picture were incapable
of ever reaching the noble status of innateness simply because
there was no special peripheral involvement. Secondary depth
cues were thus automatically considered "empirical" cues
based on associative learning. A special philosophical lure
is attached to this controversy by the fact that nativism is
a distant — or perhaps not so distant — relative of rational-

ism, and that in turn rationalism remained the dominant philosophy on the European Continent. The paradoxical situation thus arose that rationalism was implicitly served by what could be called peripheral "physiologism," bespeaking the elevation in scientific prestige accorded at least temporarily to the hitherto belittled surface region of the organism.

The second tactical classification of the depth criteria may be passed over briefly. It is given by the distinction between monocular and binocular cues. Only accommodation switches position under this new scheme. But again the major category of order is the involvement versus the irrelevance of a peripheral receptor organ.

The third tactical classification is in terms of the sensory system involved. Here the visual cues are juxtaposed to the nonvisual, notably to the "tactile-kinesthetic" cues. Only convergence and accommodation are in the latter category, while binocular disparity, the first of the original primary cues, is now grouped with the secondary criteria. Classification of psychological events in terms of the sensory system to which they belong must be considered, even though still prevalent in many texts, another relic of nineteenth-century peripheralism.

Beginnings of Ecological Analysis

Let us now turn to the treatment of cues in terms of the environmental or ecological portion of the mediating process. The emphasis on this external portion is present in much of traditional speculative physiognomics. Coming back to our example from Aristotle, we note that the statement is concerned primarily with the alleged fact that foxlike features are in reality associated with foxlike character, and only secondarily with the problem of whether or not this sign is being picked up or "utilized" by the perceiver; it is not at all concerned with the details of how such utilization may work in the way of tactical technicality, that is, what the nervous pathways organizing the impact may be like. The same holds for Gall's phrenology or the more recent constitutional typologies.

What is new in these latter attempts may be classified

under two main headings. One concerns the machinery by which the association between distal variable and cue comes about; if you will permit my subordinating this machinery under the over-all purposive unity of the cognitive act, we may call this the ecological tactics of the cue. The second concerns the degree of association between distal variable and cue. As we have observed earlier, historical attempts show a predilection for making absolute the object-cue relationship, as if we were dealing with a kind of language emitted by the object in accordance with the strict rules observed by a rational being when engaged in speaking. Newer attempts realize that the voice of nature is not quite like the voice of reason; they recognize that nature may scatter its effects more irregularly. Definite limitations in what we have called the ecological validity of a cue are thus being more readily admitted.

Concern with ecological tactics and concern with ecological validity are of course intimately interwoven. If we know the machinery of a cue, we may at the same time realize that other machineries may produce the same cue without being backed by the same distal event; by the same token, we may learn how to "fake" the cue, that is, how to create a misleading instance artificially. In other words, we will realize that in the general case we will have to treat cognition as based on equivocal rather than univocal sign–significate relationships or, as Thurstone once said about perception, as based on insufficient evidence.

Ecological validity is a statistical concept based on the principles of contingency or correlation and requiring the cool-headed gathering of a representative array of information. In the general case it involves the integration of both positive and negative, confirming and disconfirming (misleading) instances of concomitance of the distal variable with the cue variable. Small wonder, then, that in the discovery of the limitations of ecological validity the more casuistic study of "exceptions" to the rule comes first; among them, those exceptions that can be produced artificially have exerted particular attraction, perhaps as a result of the same dialectics that marks the switch from the absolutism of naïve realism to the utter negativism of the skeptics.

Turning to the depth cues again, we find that among the various classifications proposed in listing them there is one which is unashamedly based on the possibility of ecological "faking." This is the designation of certain cues as "painter's cues," that is, those configurations which the painter may use to create the impression of depth without depth being actually present. It will be remembered that the description of these cues was one of Leonardo's pet subjects, far antedating the various types of description in terms of organismic tactics which we have listed above. In terms of these later classification schemes the painter's cues encompass all cues except the binocular cues and those involving motion.

An early example of the fact that cues conceived primarily in peripheral tactical terms during the nineteenth century were originally looked upon with an eye more on the ecology is given by the cue of accommodation. In terms of classical nineteenth-century analysis this is a primary, monocular, kinesthetic cue. But in Berkeley's *New Theory of Vision* of 1709 the cue appears under the label of "blurredness," referring to the lack of sharpness of objects out of focus as contrasted with the sharpness of the objects in proper focus. The emphasis is on the proximal retinal image and its ecological history rather than on the peripheral machinery within the organism. Since the blurredness of the object out of focus is as much a confirming instance of the cue as is the sharpness of the object in proper focus, the present example does not involve limitations in the ecological validity of the cue, however.

Cues as Proximal Variables

In the same vein we may insert another remark merely reflecting on the neglect of ecological consideration in classical experimental psychology. Ideally, the most appropriate cutting-in level in the definition of a distance cue appears to be the proximal level. Blurredness versus sharpness of the retinal image, if offered without further commentary, is an example of a purely proximal definition of a cue variable. But we notice that in many of the current textbook designations of depth cues — the word "designation" is used here in contradistinction to "classification" (which is usually peripheral) — proximal and ecological aspects are intertwined in a rather unhappy confusion.

For example, we hear of a cue variously labeled as "interception," "interposition," "covering," or "overlapping." All these terms refer to the ecological history of the retinal image, indicating that a nearer object blocks out part of a farther object. Without exception, the examples offered for operation of the cue involve objects of some intrinsic regularity, such as circular discs, rectangles, boxes, and so on. It soon becomes evident that the retinal situation involves the disruption of what Wertheimer has called the "good continuation" of the contours of these overlapped objects. The proximal nature of the cue would thus most aptly be described as "poor continuation (coupled with good continuation and completeness of an intersecting object)." The recent experiments by Ratoosh (24) and by Chapanis and McCleary (5) on the utilization of this cue confirm this interpretation in terms of Gestalt factors. Describing the cue by such ecological terms as "overlapping" or "interception" involves the same absolute view of the cue that underlies Aristotle's case of foxlike appearance; it tacitly implies that the characteristic combination of poor with good continuation to which we have just referred is *always* the result of a three-dimensional arrangement, with the object that shows good continuation in front and the object that shows poor continuation in the back. In reality, the so-called interception cue is a painter's cue and thus one that can be reproduced on a flat surface; in addition, an objectively moon-shaped object could well be combined with an object in the shape of a frying-pan in such a way that the former is in reality in front of the latter and neither is in reality characterized by good continuation, thus furnishing a misleading instance of the cue.

Perhaps more than anyone else, it was Gibson (11) who helped to free the definition of the perceptual depth cues from its unrecognized entanglement with ecology. His definitions, notably those in terms of "retinal gradients," are clearly focused on the proximal geometry per se. Gibson's own "expanse" cue, describing the rapid increase in the size of the retinal image of a landing airplane, might well have become known by some such name as the "approach" cue if the sloppy traditional labeling practices had been followed, thus nipping in the bud the analysis of the interrelationships between cue and ecology.

Classification of Cues in Terms of Ecological Validity. Representative Design

But the separation of issues effected by Gibson, while an important step in the right direction, constitutes but one of the preconditions for the execution of textural ecology and its rescue from absolutism. When I began some fifteen years ago to realize the urgency for the analysis of depth cues of this latter task, along with its formidable proportions, nothing but some physiognomic studies existed to point the way. These latter shared with the casuistic treatment of misleading instances of depth cues of which we have spoken above a rather markedly negativistic attitude. These studies involved correlational statistics, to be sure, and were on rather solid ground; but in claiming low or zero correlations between physical and mental characteristics such leading authors in the field as Donald G. Paterson (23) or Cleeton and Knight (6) unmistakably revealed their gusto and delight in exploding the myths of physiognomics. Again, the pendulum swings from naïve realism to utter skepticism. While this may to a certain extent be justified in physiognomics, it certainly does not hold true for depth perception. Here we know almost offhand that many of the depth cues will be fairly dependable, but we would like to know just exactly how dependable they are.

Perhaps the greatest boon to be gained from correlational physiognomics was the realization of the fact that any investigation in textural ecology inherently requires sampling from a population or universe. In the case of the objects of physiognomic perception this requirement was as good as automatic, because the actual or potential social objects involved were themselves persons and thus fell within the traditional domain of application of the sampling practices. But this precedent did not hold for the universe of situations involving depth perception. It thus had to be newly postulated that ecological objects or situations, even if not persons, should be representatively sampled: only by such "representative design" would we be enabled to estimate the over-all ecological validities inherent in the texture of a certain ecological universe or subuniverse. To approximate roughly such representativeness, pictures from *Life* magazine were at first selected. Instances involving a rather broad variety of depth cues were analyzed, and the corresponding real depths were intellectually reconstructed as well as possible from the context of the picture. It turned out that on the basis of this preliminary evidence so-called interception was perhaps the ecologically most valid of all depth cues; that is to say, of all the characteristic intertwinings of poor with good continuation of which we have spoken above as characterizing the cue proximally (and in a picture), practically all instances were traceable to objective depth arrangements with the poor-continuation object in the back rather than in front. Binocular disparity, in the eyes of nineteenth-century psychology the monarch of the distance cues, seemed a poor second by comparison; its ecological validity is marred by the fact that in all photographic reproduction of three-dimensional reality the cue suggests two-dimensionality. (In our special case, the presence of pictures within the pictures was considered for this part of the analysis, whereas the magazine pictures themselves were treated as if given in three dimensions.) For the obviously less valid depth cues, known as vertical position, space-filling (number of distinguishable steps between objects), and color, Seidner (26) has done a series of more thorough investigations and has come out with significant ecological validities ranging up to .4.

One of the great merits of the school of Gestalt psychology is the fact that it has called our attention to the presence of so-called tacit presuppositions in our science. We all are familiar with the famed "constancy hypothesis," an unverbalized presupposition inherent in classical nineteenth-century psychology, according to which sensations are univocally related to the elements of peripheral excitation. The original constancy hypothesis thus is a peripheral–central assumption. We may suspect, however, that other regions too may be interconnected by surreptitious constancy hypotheses. For example, the point may be made that ignoring the problem of ecological validity bespeaks the presence of a distal–proximal constancy hypothesis so far as the depth cues are concerned. This suspicion is confirmed by the fact that a physical law is frequently invoked as underlying the operation of a cue: for example, the law of triangulation or the various laws of physical optics. Such reference to law implies a tendency to forget that general laws become univocal predictors only if further specifications concerning the particulars of the mediating strata — such as the presence or absence of lenses or screens — is made. True enough that the "faking" of cues in consequence of contingencies or artificialities along this line is recognized as a possibility, and in fact is generously employed as a device of experimental analysis. Yet in the classification of cues we search in vain for an indication of a hierarchical conception as to their signification potential. Ecological classification is not entirely absent in classical experimental space psychology, to be sure. But we find it confined to relatively secondary considerations, such as the distinction between cues operating best at small versus large distances (say, binocular disparity as against so-called aerial perspective) or between cues giving a metric indication of depth as opposed to those merely indicating order (say, binocular disparity as opposed to interception). As to dependability in the sense of relative frequency of positive versus misleading instances, cues tend to be tacitly treated as if on a par in absolute perfection. Their status in the eyes of classical psychology thus resembles somewhat that of an unquestioned social stereotype as formed by the man on the street: unthinkingly made absolute yet often misleading.

Cue Utilization and Its Vicariousness

One of the effects of this oversimplified picture of the ecology was a crippling of the scope of the problems of organismic strategy. These problems should be handled in close contact with those of ecological validity. Proper cognitive adjustment demands (a) that vicarious utilization of many cues be present when validities are imperfect, and (b) that hierarchy of utilization (relative strength in rivalry) follow hierarchy of validity. Neither vicariousness nor rivalry can thus be properly understood without the fact of limited ecological validity.

This is the more to be noted, as we know, from other fields and from the over-all theory of psychology that vicarious functioning is one of the most fundamental principles, if not *the* most fundamental principle, of behavior. When Hunter (16) introduced the term, this was done in search of a definition of the subject matter of psychology, and in the status of the defining criterion. In effect, vicarious functioning plays the major role in the definitions by McDougall (22) and by Tolman (28) of the purposiveness of behavior. Hull (15) has incorporated it in his theory of the habit-family-hierarchy, a theory that was never surpassed as to level of complexity in his subsequent work. Psychoanalytic mechanisms are an expression of vicarious functioning; in her work on the interrelationships between motivation and overt behavior, Else Frenkel-Brunswik (8) has given quantitative expression to the possibility of "alternative manifestations" of common underlying drives, thus projecting onto an operational plane the psychoanalytic distinction between the latent and the manifest, and the vicariousness in their interrelationship.

Vicarious functioning encompasses both the divergent and the convergent part of the lenslike patterns that characterize all achievement. In the field of cognition, it is the divergent part — ecological validity — which is ecological and the convergent part — utilization — which is organismic. While isolative or absolute experiments on the utilization of depth cues have a long history, experiments in the relative utilization or rivalry of depth cues came into their own but thirty years ago;

none of them have so far pitted cues against each other under the principles of representative design. But at least some good evidence has been assembled on the fact that binocular disparity can be overpowered by interception or by combinations of other cues, quite as it should be in view of its limited validity, at least in a cultural ecology.

Parallel problems arise in the field of physiognomics and social perception. Vicariousness is predicated upon limited ecological validity and in turn raises the problem of rivalry in utilization. A wide area of the pathology of cue-utilization is thus opened up, development of which may profit from the academic theory of depth perception as it may from its more indigenous roots in personality psychology. That the proper recognition of the vicarious functioning of cues may be one of the chief incentives for the introduction of representative design into the diagnostic process has been pointed out by Hammond (12). Hammond and his collaborators at Colorado also are among the pioneers in the study of the pathology of mediation in the diagnostician. A monograph by Smedslund (27) in Oslo on the probability learning of multiple cues illuminates the selective or distortive use of artificial cue systems in neurotics or in those who, in the terminology of Frenkel-Brunswik (9), show extreme "intolerance of ambiguity."

Ratiomorphic Explication of the Cognitive Process. Gestalt Principles and Probability Learning

On the other hand, it must also be granted that an element of maladaptiveness and thus, in a sense, of pathology, is intrinsic to any utilization of cues that are not perfectly dependable. As in any stereotype or as in wagering, there must always be what Reichenbach has called a "posit," that is, an implicit perceptual hypothesis; yet this hypothesis will be wrong in all the misleading instances of the cue. It may be helpful to try to explicate these underlying hypotheses in a rational manner or, in brief, to develop what may be called a "ratiomorphic" (3) theory of perceptual utilization. In essence this would constitute an expansion of Helmholtz's doctrine of unconscious inference (14). In the days of Gestalt psychology it would have taken some defensive argument before one could have revived such skeletons in the closet. In our day of "hypotheses in rats" (21), of information theory, of calculating machines, of the open recognition of "teleological mechanisms" (1), and of the explicit comparison of nervous activity with two-valued logic, such defensiveness seems no longer necessary.

All ratiomorphic explication must take recourse to some form of regularity or law. As we have anticipated, physical law seems readily available to serve as a template for the explication of the primary depth cues; along with ready physiological identifiability this is perhaps partly why these cues were singled out from the others.

More intriguing and more rewarding from the point of view of our understanding of perception is the ratiomorphic explication of the so-called secondary cues. This may be undertaken by pinning down those ecological conditions under which the cue would be ideally correct. For example, the cue of interception would be ecologically fully valid if all object contours were in reality characterized by good continuation. Its implicit hypothesis is therefore, briefly, that all objects are of regular shape; perception behaves *as if* good continuation were a universal natural law. Similarly, linear perspective and Gibson's density- or texture-gradients work on the assumption that all objects appearing to be otherwise equal, such as telephone poles, trees, railroad ties, brush, or pebbles on a beach, are in reality equal in size as well. Or the cue of vertical position is predicated on the assumption that we are looking at objects below the horizon which are of equal objective elevation. And, finally, the light-and-shade cue operates, at least predominantly, as if it were a law that light comes from above rather than from below.

Some of the explicated hypotheses would seem to be readily subsumable under the well known principles of Gestalt organization, usually encompassed by the law of pregnance. But obviously such factors as light-and-shade distribution or some of the assumptions underlying the vertical position cue demand a more empirical interpretation. In collaboration with Kamiya (4) it could be established that at least one of the allegedly autochthonous Gestalt factors, "nearness" in the visual field, possesses at least a modicum of ecological validity with respect to distal object manipulability. It thus seems that an interpretation fitting all cues or organization principles could best be derived by assuming that their underlying hypotheses are the outcome of some generalizing type of probability learning rather than of principles intrinsic to Gestalt dynamics.

Ratiomorphic explication is but one of several aspects of the utilization problem, that is, of the intraorganismic leg of the cognitive process. While the sheer fact of utilization may seem to yield to "explanation" in terms of mediational technology, ratiomorphic explication deals, as we have just argued, with the underlying rationale of cognition in a way that cannot be divorced from the ecological leg of the process. It is only by comparing the reconstructed perceptual hypotheses with the ecological validities that their character mentioned above as crude overgeneralizations or stereotypes is revealed. It is obvious at once that they not only fail to represent universal law; they do not even represent ecological or local law so long as the term "law" is used in the usual, strict sense.

The picture of the cognitive absolutism of the perceptual system which we have just drawn holds only so long as we assume an unmitigated exploitation of the cue on the part of the responding system. But such radical response is in reality not the case. The facts of rivalry and compromise to which we have referred above suggest that cues will yield to conflicting evidence, perhaps even in an ecologically rather well adjusted "hierarchy" of relative utilization strength. In the light of this, all the above perceptual hypotheses should be reformulated as involving not absolute law but relative frequency.

Distribution Hypotheses and Correlation Hypotheses in Perception

At this point we are reminded of certain previous uses of the term "perceptual hypothesis," notably in the framework of the so-called hypothesis-information theory of perception proposed by Bruner (2) and by Postman (25). Some of their experiments on the subject center about the theme that certain stimuli or configurations occur more frequently than others and therefore are more readily perceived. Possibly Gibson's (10) observation about the progressively decreasing apparent curvature of curved lines under prolonged observation, or some of Köhler and Wallach's (20) figural displacements could be similarly explicated as a refusal on the part of perception to accept infrequent facts or relationships, although I doubt that the authors would agree with such ratiomorphic reformulation. Ivo Kohler's (19) observation that for persons wearing special systems of lenses, familiar letters tend to remain in their normal orientation, even if left-right reversal is effective in the rest of the field, belongs in the same category.

The facts listed in the preceding paragraph have in common that they involve what may be called "distribution hypotheses," that is, expectations regarding frequencies along a single dimension (or a set of isolated dimensions), as revealed by perceptual belief in the recurrence of the probable in accordance with past distribution and by mounting perceptual disbelief in the face of a serious threat toward an upsetting of this distribution. In this latter respect there is a resemblance to Jarvik's (17) "negative recency effect," a case similar to the so-called "gambler's fallacy." Here too there is increasing skepticism concerning the future occurence of what is generally rare, even though — or even because — it has been prevalent in the immediately preceding series of events.

The case of depth cues, on the other hand, involves "correlation hypotheses." Although the hypotheses underlying cue utilization are in the nature of distribution hypotheses in the above unidimensional sense (say, concerning the prevalence of good continuation in our nature-culture), they are not really put to test in the experimental situation, as is the case for the experiments just cited. Rather, they are developed, in a series of experiential or quasilogical steps, in to some bidimensional sign–significate hypotheses (in our example, concerning the indicative power of poor as against good continuation with respect to depth); and the testing of these hypotheses, if it is to take place at all, lies in the more distant future. The old semantic criterion for sign function, "something stands for something else," is fulfilled only in the case of a correlation hypothesis; the cue itself is not challenged from the frequency point of view, but what is involved is merely the frequency of its association with the significate. Only correlation hypotheses are able really to venture out into the distal environment and thus to become related to the problems of textural ecology as we have defined them; distribution hypotheses and the study of their effects must in the nature of things remain essentially proximal in character.

The Crippling of the Cognitive Problem by Tied-variable Designs. Encapsulation Within the Skin

Above we have spoken of the pathology of the perceiver. There also is a pathology of the science that deals with the perceiver. Pathology is not meant in any grossly dramatic sense here; we merely wish to point out that there may be in the design of cognitive research certain unrealistic and perhaps formalistic predilections that narrow our scope of the problem. At least some of them are traceable to the all-or-none absolutism regarding ecological validity of which we have spoken above.

Systematic psychological experiments involving depth perception may be grouped into two major categories, those thriving on a confirming instance of the cue under neglect of the misleading case, and those thriving on the misleading case at the neglect of the confirming case. In the most recent experimental work on perception the former, apparently more positive policy is represented by some, although by no means all, of the work of Gibson, while the latter is predominant in the work of Ames and the Princeton group. Sometimes the declared aim is to study the utilization of cues, notably in the misleading-case type of distortive experiment that provokes gross illusion. Sometimes the declared aim is to study the problem of achievement, that is, that most encompassing type of cognitive problem that takes us back to the beginning of our considerations. Perceptual size constancy is such a problem. Gibson has reported on experiments in which size constancy was practically perfect (11, Chap. 9). But closer inspection of his experimental design reveals that he had chosen his experimental conditions so as to represent an idealized rather than the real ecology. By performing his experiment in an open field with even texture and density he artificially made absolute, in the temporary subecology of his experiment, the "law" presumed by the perceptual hypothesis underlying the utilization of the cue. In the terminology of representative design he thus artificially tied — that is, confounded to a perfect degree — the distal and the proximal variables. Size constancy is automatic in this case, or it is an artifact of the design, provided that the cue is being utilized by the organism. That is to say, the experiment has no distal relevance; it does not really venture out into the ecology. All it does is to test the utilization of the cue, which is a purely intraorganismic problem. Idealization of the ecology thus leads to encapsulation of research within the skin.

The Princetonians, on the other hand, have a distinguished line of ancestry to the so-called "transdermal transactionism" of John Dewey and Arthur F. Bentley (7), which would seem to commit them to a search for genuinely distal research policies. But just as Gibson's rose-colored experiments, as we have seen, do not really pierce the skin, the Princetonians' bleakly distortive experiments do not pierce the skin either. In terms of representative design, theirs is a policy in which cue variable and distal variable are tied inversely, creating *ad hoc* a perfect negative ecological validity. These experiments, too, merely probe into cue utilization, that is, into strategy and mechanism, stressing the negative side of achievement but failing to reflect it proportionately.

If tested under representative situational conditions, size constancy is high but not absolute as measured in correlational terms; in other words, relatively high accuracy is the rule but there are large exceptions. So long as the cognitive problem is kept in mind in its full scope, such a probabilistic approach in terms of a mapping of functional validities is the only adequate approach to the problem of accuracy of achievement.

In another paper, Dr. Osgood provides a cogent analysis of the riddles of the "little black box," as we like to fancy the intraorganismic world in general and the nervous system in particular to be. What we have attempted to show here is that there also are riddles of what most of us have tended to treat as a "big white box," or, still better, a "big open box"; that is, our surroundings. Since physics has taught us the most universal laws of the external world, and geography provides the particulars, no exigencies seem to be left. But as it is the intermediate level of generality which provides the little black box with problems all its own, the ecology too is full of particular semiregularities all its own to which we have become somewhat blinded by the shining streaks of light of the purely nomothetic approach. As we have seen especially in the ratiomorphic explication of some of the secondary depth criteria, the cognitive system struggles hard to get hold of just these intermediate generalities. As we may gather from the psychology of learning, *ad hoc* regularities of limited spatial or temporal scope, or even of but partial validity, are the bread of the adjusting organism; the general laws of physics are more like the butter which none but the most highly developed strata of the cognitive system can afford.

Or to say this still differently: in the psychological applications of communication theory it is usually the organism that appears as the source of noise; in reality, however, the limited ecological validities of proximal cues relative to distal object variables furnish a perfect environmental counterpart to this internal noise. The translation of depth into depth cues is a case of probabilistic encoding even though this encoding takes place by virtue of the causal chains of nature-culture rather than by virtue of human fiat. Osgood's scheme begins with the decoding on the part of the organism of the messages from the environment, that is, with what we call utilization. Should it not then be recognized that equal attention must be given to the predicaments of the encoding process, a process which of necessity must precede any decoding? Only in this manner can

the textural analogies between the macrocosm of the environment and the microcosm of the organism be developed and
utilized to the best advantage of psychology.

To sum up: while philosophy and other antecedents of psychology have set the broad framework of the cognitive problem, starting from the most encompassing aspect of achievement and remaining aware of environmental texture when
working down to organismic strategy, psychology proper took
the reverse course, beginning with the microproblems of cognitive tactics and tending to encapsulate within the organism.
We have tried to show that only by detailed analysis of ecological textures can the cognitive problem be restored from mere
utilization problems to its full scope of achievement problems
and thus again become the key to the core question of psychology, that of the adjustment of the organism to a complex
environment.

BIBLIOGRAPHY

1. *Annals of the New York Academy of Science*. Vol. 50, No. 4 (1948).
2. Blake, R. R., and G. V. Ramsey (eds.) *Perception — An Approach to Personality*. New York: Ronald (1951).
3. Brunswik, E. Ratiomorphic models of perception and thinking. *Proc. 14th Internat. Congress Psychol.*, ed. by M. Mailloux. Montreal (1954).
4. Brunswik, E., and J. Kamiya. Ecological cue-validity of "proximity" and of other Gestalt factors. *Amer. J. Psychol.*, 66:20–32 (1953).
5. Chapanis, A., and R. A. McCleary. Interposition as a cue for the perception of relative distance. *J. gen. Psychol.*, 48:113–132 (1953).
6. Cleeton, G. U., and F. B. Knight. Validity of character judgments based on external criteria. *J. appl. Psychol.*, 8:215–231 (1924).
7. Dewey, J., and A. F. Bentley. *Knowing and the Known*. Boston: Beacon Press (1949).
8. Frenkel-Brunswik, E. Motivation and behavior. *Genet. Psychol. Monogr.*, 26:121–265 (1942).
9. Frenkel-Brunswik, E. Intolerance of ambiguity as an emotional and perceptual personality variable. *J. Pers.*, 18:108–143 (1949).
10. Gibson, J. J. Adaptation, after-effect, & contrast in the perception of curved lines. *J. exper. Psychol.*, 16:1–31 (1933).
11. Gibson, J. J. *The Perception of the Visual World*. Boston: Houghton Mifflin (1950).

12. Hammond, K. R. Probabilistic functioning and the clinical method. *Psychol. Rev.*, 62:255–262 (1955).

13. Heider, F. Environmental determinants in psychological theories. *Psychol. Rev.*, 46:383–410 (1939).

14. Helmholtz, H. *Handbuch der physiologischen Optik*, Vol. 3, 1866; trans. from 3d ed. by J. P. C. Southall. Rochester: Opt. Soc. of Amer. (1925).

15. Hull, C. L. The concept of the habit-family-hierarchy and maze learning. *Psychol. Rev.*, 41:33–54 and 134–154 (1934).

16. Hunter, W. S. *Human Behavior.* Chicago: Univ. of Chicago Press (1928).

17. Jarvik, M. E. Probability learning and a negative recency effect in the serial anticipation of alternative symbols. *J. exp. Psychol.*, 41: 291–297 (1951).

18. Koffka, K. *Principles of Gestalt Psychology.* New York: Harcourt Brace (1935).

19. Kohler, I. *Über Aufbau und Wandlungen der Wahrnehmungswelt.* Vienna: Rohrer (1951).

20. Köhler, W., and H. Wallach. Figural after-effects: an investigation of visual processes. *Proc. Amer. Phil. Soc.*, 88:269–357 (1944).

21. Krechevsky, I. Hypotheses in rats. *Psychol. Rev.*, 39:516–532 (1932).

22. McDougall, W. *Introduction to Social Psychology.* London: Methuen (1908).

23. Paterson, D. G. *Physique and Intellect.* New York: Appleton-Century (1930).

24. Ratoosh, P. On interposition as a cue for the perception of distance. *Proc. Nat. Acad. Sci.*, Wash., 35:257–259 (1949).

25. Rohrer, J. H., and M. Sherif. (eds.) *Social Psychology at the Crossroads.* New York: Harper (1951).

26. Seidner, S. E. Ecological validity of visual depth criteria. Univ. of California doctoral dissertation (in progress).

27. Smedslund, J. *Multiple-probability Learning.* Oslo: Akademisk Forlag (1955).

28. Tolman, E. C. *Purposive Behavior in Animals and Men.* New York: Century (1932).

DISCUSSION
C. E. Osgood

I DO NOT envy Fritz Heider his task of interrelating the other papers in this symposium and discerning general trends — not that the job is impossible, but it certainly is a difficult one. Brunswik, Bruner, Osgood, Festinger, and Rapaport are concerned with the common problem of cognitive process, but, as you will find, with quite different emphases and with quite different levels of analysis in the constructs employed. And there is a translation problem: we all use rather different languages for talking about cognition. In many cases I am sure that adequate translations are going to reveal that we are saying approximately the same things in different terms; in other, more confusing cases I am afraid we will be found to be using the same terms from our common psychological vocabulary, but with subtly different connotations. In any case, I think one of the most useful things we shall be able to do in our discussions will be to try to translate back and forth among our several languages, thereby removing purely terminological blockades and building bridges between us.

In order to get what for me was the full flavor of Professor Brunswik's paper, and to appreciate its impact, I first had to translate — sometimes easily and surely and at other times with difficulty and uncertainty. At the risk of being obscure because I have not yet presented my own paper, but to facilitate the translation I think we require, let me first suggest some of the relationships I see between Brunswik's notions and my own behavioristic ones.

Central in his thinking is the notion that both thing-perception and social perception involve "cognitive attainment" of "distal variables" or objects on the basis of independently variable "proximal cues" or sensory input. Now, I think Brunswik would agree that "proximal" input is equivalent to "stimulus" in the strict sense of the term. I think he would also agree with me in saying that such "proximal" stimulation may *or may not* be utilized in "cognitive attainment," and that when it is so utilized the proximal stimulation is functioning as a *sign*. Now, in my own paper, I shall define a sign as any stimulus acquiring association with a *representational* mediation process, representational because its nature is dependent upon some other stimulus with which the sign has been associated. This other stimulus, or *significate* in my terms, is I believe roughly equivalent to Brunswik's "distal object." In other words, I would say that certain proximal cues acquire the capacity to signify certain distal objects via some such mechanism as this, and that this formation of signifying processes is the essence of cognition or "cognitive attainment" in Brunswik's sense. One thing I miss in Brunswik's paper is an explicit analysis of just how this signifying relation develops: for example, how proximal cues do come to represent or signify things other than themselves, or how distal variables are mapped into central or cognitive events in the organism. If this gap does exist in his model, it may be that our two systems can be fruitfully related to one another at this point. There are certain problems about the psychological meaning of "distal variable" in his paper to which I shall return later.

Another point of fruitful contact between Brunswik's system and the one I shall describe arises in his notion of the variable "functional validity" of proximal cues. If I read him right, by this he means that a particular proximal cue may be to varying degrees an ambiguous sign with respect to a particular distal object; or, perhaps better, that the same proximal cue may become a sign of several distal objects to varying degrees, depending upon the past history of probabilistic learning. This is strictly equivalent to the notion of habit-family-hierarchy as I shall use it, according to which a particular sign

becomes associated with a hierarchy of representational mediators (for example, meanings), but to varying degrees. Brunswik himself noted this correspondence in his paper. This, of
course, would be what I call a divergent hierarchy and hence
one in which one expects competition.

Along the same lines, a variety or class of proximal stimuli
can become signs of the *same* object; for example, they can
become associated with a common mediation process. Specifically, in relation to perceptual significance problems, I shall
try to show how perceptual constancy is a case in which a
graduated series of physically similar stimuli (proximal cues)
become associated with a common signifying process. In depth
perception, as Professor Brunswik so clearly shows, we have a
case in which a class of physically *dissimilar* proximal cues
become associated with a common representational process
(the surrogate of the distal object). Certainly, proprioceptive
feedback from the ocular muscles, visual disparity derived
from the binocular system, a shading cue, a partial masking
cue, and a particular retinal size cue have little in common as
physical inputs to the sensory system, yet they do signify
something in common about the distance of an object from the
observer.

In this connection Brunswik uses a term which I also use —
but I am sure he means quite different things by it. He refers
to the "vicarious functioning" of such proximal cues as these
signifying depth and distance. My own use of this term stems
from neurophysiology, particularly in destruction experiments
where one may say that one brain region can function vicariously for the other when that other is eliminated. Now, I
think Brunswik means more than the mere substitution of one
proximal cue for another in depth perception, say — rather, I
think he refers to the complex interaction, facilitation, summation, interference, and so on, among such sets of proximal cues,
the operations of which we would each describe in our own
terms. For this reason I find the term "vicarious functioning"
confusing in this context. Another instance where we use the
same term with quite different reference is the word "mediation": Brunswik uses mediation to refer, as I read him, to

the entire sequence from proximal–distal relations, through intraorganismic processes, peripheral to central to motor, to relations between organism behavior and distal object; I shall use mediation to refer strictly to an intraorganismic process. I point these differences out to avoid possible confusions later on.

I was particularly interested in the discussion in this paper of relations *between* proximal and distal variables. Brunswik refers to "ecological validity" as the probability with which a particular proximal cue actually indexes the presence of a particular distal object. He also refers to "ecological strategy" as a purely intraenvironmental operation of objectively noting the relations between cues and objects, presumably by physical operations of one sort or another. The demonstration by the Princeton people that the same retinal image can be produced by an infinite series of physical arrangements, for example, in the distorted room geometries, would presumably be a case of this. This, of course, is not psychology — but there are lots of nonpsychological things that psychologists do for very good psychological reasons. However, in Brunswik's analysis of intraecological relations, between proximal cues and distal objects and presumably independent of the organism itself, one runs into what I think *is* a serious question: just what *are* "distal variables" apart from the organism? When we compute relations between physical locations and sizes of visual angles of an object, say a tree-stump or a playing card, why do we segregate the tree-stump from a bush behind it, the playing card from the hand that holds it? It seems to me that something other than purely physical considerations tells us what to include or exclude from both the distal object and the proximal cue. It seems to me that proximal cues are ambiguous with respect to distal objects only when we have some criteria for stating when distal events are the same or different; it is only because human organisms identify as "the same" an apple under various illuminations that hue is an ambiguous cue for object color; it is only because human organisms identify as "different" large apples and little apples that retinal size is an ambiguous cue as to the distal object.

There is another interesting problem that comes up in relation to "distal variables." I was pleased to find that Brunswik, unlike some of his secondary sources, was very careful not to speak of "distal *cues*" in contrast to "proximal cues," because this would be confusing in the extreme. The distal object is necessarily a construct inferred from a variety of proximal stimulations. To be sure, we discover that "apples" are roundish, tangy to the taste, juicy, texturally smooth, and gratifying — but these too are proximal stimuli. I take it this is what Professor Brunswik meant when he reiterated Kant's question as to whether the "thing in itself" is ever knowable. I think this is a pseudo-problem — because any criterion of what things *really* are must be arbitrary and relative to some contestable frame of reference or measurement operation. But we do have a problem here — what, as far as the behaving organism is concerned, is the distal object? I have my own kind of answer to this question — essentially that certain proximal cues (like the apple-in-the-mouth) are capable of reliably eliciting certain behaviors (like salivating, chewing, digesting) and when other proximal cues acquire capacity to elicit a representational portion of these behaviors, they become *signs* of the other cues (for example, the sight of the apple becomes a sign of something edible, texturally smooth, gratifying, and the like). In other words, although the distal object "apple" may be identified by physical operations, *distal variables in behavior* are representational processes derived from the behavior of organisms to certain proximal cues these objects excite.

I also might note in passing that Brunswik has limited himself to those two classes of proximal cues which I would call "natural signs" and "significates." Natural signs, which would include the smoke-as-a-sign-of-fire cases as well as all perceptual signs, like masking as a sign of relative distance, have a necessary physical dependency relation to their significates. On the other hand, the human organism employs a great number of signs that bear a completely arbitrary, socially-assigned relation to the things they signify. These, of course, include linguistic signs and many other arbitrary symbols. The noises "house" and "mouse" are physically similar but have reference to quite different things. Brunswik does not discuss signs of this type, and of course there is no reason why he should. But linguistic signs also operate as proximal cues in auditory and visual modalities and, I suspect, acquire their relationships to distal objects in essentially the same way that perceptual signs do — except for the fact that they do not have any physical dependency upon the distal objects they represent.

There are two final comments of a more general sort I would like to make. The first is a reaction to Brunswik's emphasis upon the need for representative ecological sampling of objects and situations as well as subjects in testing psychological principles. Although I had taken due note of this quite a few years ago, the full significance and importance of this strategy didn't bear in on me until, in my own factor-analytic work on the measurement of meaning, I discovered that the kind of semantic factors one derives from subjects depends to a great extent upon the sample of objects these subjects are judging. In other words, there is a definite interaction between concept judged and subject doing the judging in determining what correlations will be found between dimensions or scales of judgment. If a person samples objects of judgment solely from the political frame of reference, for example, he discovers that potency (*strong–weak*) is highly correlated with evaluation (*good–bad*); if he samples concrete physical objects, on the other hand, these two dimensions of meaning tend to be independent. For this reason, we have tried to sample objects of judgment representatively and broadly in our semantic factor work.

My last point concerns Brunswik's early statement that if there is anything that ails psychology, it is the neglect of investigation of ecological or environmental texture. I think I know the cause of this ailment. It is simply that psychologists have not as yet solved the problem of the *descriptive units* of their science — in fact, they haven't worried about it much. By what criteria or operations do we identify our stimuli and responses, or, perhaps better, the unitary situation and the unitary act? In practice we act like laymen — "a bush," "a choice-point," "a smiling face" are unitary situations because we have names in our language for such things; "shaking hands," "turning left," "avoiding it" are unitary acts because, again, our language provides us with ways of carving up behavior as well as situations. But this is a very intuitive and informal kind of operation.

Interestingly enough, there is one segment of psychology in which these operations in ecological unit-making have been carried out with exhaustiveness and rigor. This area is language, and those who have carried out this descriptive job are linguists, not psychologists. I think the psychologist can take a hint from the linguist and perhaps do a better job than previously in making units of the rest of the psychological domain. The linguist identifies two major levels of units: *phonemes* (which are meaningless in themselves but serve as basic *discriminanda*) and *morphemes* (which are the smallest meaningful units). The former correspond to what I shall call in my paper sensory and motor integrations; the latter, I think, correspond to units defined by the significances and intentions of organisms. But how are such intentional and significant units in behavior to be identified?

Here again I think we can take a methodological hint from the linguist. He classifies as "the same" all segments of messages which have the same meaning in the code — without being concerned whatsoever with *what* this meaning may be. For example, the physically different endings of "walk-ed," "add-ed," and "play-ed" have the same (past-time) significance in the code and hence are members of the same morpheme class; similarly, the stems of "child" and "child-ren," of "leaf" and "leav-es," and of "foot" and "feet" have the same meaning, apart from the plural tag, and hence are members of the same morpheme class. Generalizing to behavior in all areas, I think one could say that all members of the class of physically different instrumental acts which are mediated by the same representational process (or intention) are "the same" as molar actions — thus a welcoming smile, saying, "It's good to see you," and shaking hands are functionally equivalent acts in the social interaction matrix; similarly, all members of the class of physical stimuli associated with a common representational process (or significance) for the organism are functionally "the same" as molar situations — the same examples of seeing a smile, hearing welcoming words, and seeing an outstretched hand would apply. It would certainly be a laborious task, but I think one could determine these classes of functionally equivalent situations and responses from the contingencies in a great situation-response matrix covering a representative sample of individuals from a given culture over a long enough period.

GOING BEYOND
THE INFORMATION GIVEN

Jerome S. Bruner
Harvard University

MORE than thirty years ago, Charles Spearman (1923) undertook the ambitious task of characterizing the basic cognitive processes whose operations might account for the existence of intelligence. He emerged with a triad of noegenetic principles, as he called them, the first of these being simply an affirmation that organisms are capable of apprehending the world they live in. The second and third principles provide us with our starting point. One of these, called, as you know, "the education of relations," holds that there is an immediate evocation of a sense of relation given the mental presentation of two or more things. "White" and "black" evoke "opposite" or "different." The third principle, the "education of correlates," states that in the presence of a thing and a relation one immediately educes another thing. "White" and "opposite of" evokes "black." I think that Spearman was trying to say that the most characteristic thing about mental life, over and beyond the fact that one apprehends the events of the world around one, is that one constantly goes beyond the information given. With this observation I find myself in full agreement, and it is here that my difficulties start. For, as Professor Bartlett (1951, p. 1) put it in a recent paper, ". . . whenever anybody interprets evidence from any source, and his interpretation contains characteristics that cannot be referred wholly to direct sensory observation or perception, this person thinks. The bother is that nobody has ever been able to find any case of the human use of evidence which does not include characters that run beyond what is directly observed by the senses. So, according to this, people think whenever they do anything at all with evidence. If we adopt that view we very soon find ourselves looking out upon a boundless and turbulent ocean of problems." Bother though it be, there is little else than to plunge right in.

Some Instances of Going Beyond the Information Given

It may help to begin with some rather commonplace examples of the different ways in which people go beyond information that is given to them. The first of these represents the simplest form of utilizing inference. It consists of learning the defining properties of a class of functionally equivalent objects and using the presence of these defining properties as a basis of inferring that a new object encountered is or is not an exemplar of the class. The first form of "going beyond," then, is to go beyond sense data to the class identity of the object being perceived. This is the more remarkable an achievement when the new object encountered differs from in more respects than it resembles other exemplars of the class that have been previously encountered. A speck on the horizon surmounted by a plume of smoke is identified as a ship, so too a towering transatlantic liner at its dock, so too a few schematic lines in a drawing. Given the presence of a few defining properties or cues, we go beyond them to the inference of identity. Having done so, we infer that the instance so categorized or identified has the other properties characteristic of membership in a category. Given the presence of certain cues of shape, size, and texture, we infer that the thing before us is an apple: *ergo,* it can be eaten, cut with a knife, it relates by certain prinicples of classification to other kinds of fruits, and so on. The act of rendering some given event equivalent with a class of other things, placing it in an identity class, provides then one of the most primitive forms of going beyond information given.

William James (1890) wrote picturesquely of this process, remarking that cognitive life begins when one is able to exclaim, "Hollo! Thingumbob again." The adaptive significance of this capacity for equivalence grouping is, of course, enormous. If we were to respond to each event as unique and to learn anew what to do about it or even what to call it, we would soon be swamped by the complexity of our environment. By last count, there were some 7.5 million discriminable differences in the color solid alone. Yet for most purposes we get by treating them as if there were only a dozen or two classes of colors. No two individuals are alike, yet we get by with perhaps a dozen or so "types" into which we class others. Equivalence categories or concepts are the most basic currency one can utilize in going beyond the sensory given. They are the first steps toward rendering the environment generic.

Consider a second form of going beyond the information given, one that involves learning the redundancy of the environment. I present the word, P*YC*OL*GY, and with no difficulty at all you recognize that the word is PSYCHOLOGY. Or the finding of Miller, Heise, and Lichten (1951) that words masked by noise are more easily recognized when they are in a meaningful or high-probability context than when they are presented in isolation. Indeed, the missing word in the sentence, "Dwight ———— is currently President of the United States" can be completely masked by noise and yet "recognized" correctly by anybody who knows the subject matter. Or we find that subjects in some experiments currently in progress check off about an average of thirty trait words from the Gough list as being characteristic of a person who is only described as being either "intelligent," or "independent," or "considerate." Any one of these key traits has at least thirty possible avenues for going beyond it, based on learned probabilities of what things are likely to go with what in another person. Once one learns the probability texture of the environment, one can go beyond the given by predicting its likely concomitants.

We move one step beyond such probabilistic ways of going

beyond the information given and come now to certain formal
bases for doing so. Two propositions are presented:

$$A > B$$
$$B > C$$

and with very little difficulty most people can readily go beyond to the inference that

$$A > C.$$

Or I present a series of numbers, with one missing one to be
supplied:

$$2, 4, 8, *, 32, 64$$

and as soon as you are able to see that the numbers are powers
of two, or that they represent successive doublings, you will
be able to provide the missing number 16. Or in an experiment
by Bruner, Matter, and O'Dowd, rats are taught to find their
way through a four-unit T-maze by threading the path LRLR.
Given the proper conditions (and to these we will return later),
an animal readily transfers to the mirror-image pattern of
RLRL — provided he has learned the path as an instance of
single alternation and not as a set of specific turns.

What it is that one learns when one learns to do the sort of
thing just described, whether it be learning to do syllogisms
or learning the principle of single alternation, is not easily described. It amounts to the learning of certain formal schemata
that may be fitted to or may be used to organize arrays of
diverse information. We shall use the expression *coding* to
describe what an organism does to information under such
circumstances, leaving its closer examination until later. Thus,
we can conceive of an organism capable of rendering things
into equivalence classes, capable of learning the probabilistic
relationships between events belonging to various classes, and
capable of manipulating these classes by the utilization of certain formal coding systems.

We often combine formal codes and probability codes in
making inferences beyond the data. Studies such as those by
Wilkins (1928) provide instructive examples. One finds, for

example, that a typical deduction made from the proposition "If all A are B" is that "All B are A," and to the proposition "If some A are not B" a typical conclusion is that "Some B are not A." Yet none of the subjects ever agrees with the proposition that "If all men are mammals, then all mammals are men," or with the proposal that "If some men are not criminals, then some criminals are not men." In sum, it may often be the case that "common sense" — the result of inductive learning of what is what and what goes with what in the environment — may often serve to correct less well learned formal methods of going beyond information given. In short, one may often have alternative modes of going beyond, sometimes in conflict with each other, sometimes operating to the same effect.

One final case before we turn to the difficult business of trying to specify what is involved in utilizing information in this soaring manner. This time we take a scientist, and we shall take him unprepared with a theory, which, as we know, is a rare state for both the scientist and the layman alike. He has, let us say, been working on the effects of sound sleep, and in pursuit of his inquiries has hit on the bright idea of giving his subjects a complete rest for five or six days — "just to see what happens." To add to their rest, he places them on a soft bed, covers their eyes with translucent ground-glass goggles, lulls their ears with a soft but persistent homogeneous masking noise, and in general makes life as homogeneously restful as possible for them. At the end of this time, he tests them and finds, lo and behold, that they are incapable of doing simple arithmetic problems, that they cannot concentrate, that their perceptual constancies are impaired, and so on down the list of findings that have recently been reported from McGill by Bexton, Heron, Scott (1954), and their collaborators. (Please note that the McGill investigators started with a hypothesis about sensory deprivation; our example is a fiction, but it will serve us and may even relate to our Canadian colleagues before they are through.) Once one has got some data of this order, one is in a funk unless one can go beyond them. To do so requires a theory. A theory, of course, is something we invent. If it is a good theory — a good formal or probabilistic coding system — it should permit us to go beyond the present data both retrospectively and prospectively. We go backward — turn around on our own schemata — and order data that before seemed unrelated to each other. Old loose ends now become part of a new pattern. We go forward in the sense of having new hypotheses and predictions about other things that should be but that have not been tested. When we have finished the reorganizing by means of the new theoretical coding system, everything then seems obvious, if the thing fits. We mention theory construction as a final example of coding processes largely because it highlights several points that are too easily overlooked in the simpler examples given earlier. Coding may involve inventive behavior and we must be concerned with what is involved in the construction of coding systems. And coding systems may be effective or ineffective in permitting one to go beyond information. Later we shall inquire into the conditions that make for construction of new coding systems and what may lead to the construction of adequate ones.

On Coding Systems

A coding system may be defined as a set of contingently related, nonspecific categories. It is the person's manner of grouping and relating information about his world, and it is constantly subject to change and reorganization. Bartlett's memory *schemata* are close to what is intended here, and the early work of Piaget (1930) on the child's conception of nature represents a naturalistic account of coding systems in the child.

Let it be clear that a coding system as I describe it here is a hypothetical construct. It is inferred from the nature of antecedent and consequent events. For example, in the rat experiment cited earlier, I teach an organism to wend a course that goes LRLR through a maze. *I wish to discover how the event is coded.* I transfer the animal to a maze that goes RLRL. He transfers with marked savings. I infer now that he has coded the situation as single alternation. But I must continue to test for the genericalness of the coding system used. Is it alternation in general or alternation only in spatial terms? To test this I set up a situation in the maze where the correct path is defined by taking alternate colors, now a black, now a white member of black-white pairs, without regard to their position. If there is saving here too, I assume that the original learning was coded not as positional alternation but as alternation in general. Of course, I use the appropriate control groups along the way. Note that the technique I am using is identical with the technique we use to discover whether children are learning proper codes in school. We provide training in addition, then we move on to numbers that the child has not yet added, then we move to abstract symbols like $a + a + a$ and see whether $3a$ emerges as the answer. Then we test further to see whether the child has grasped the idea of repeated addition, which we fool him by calling multiplication. We devise techniques of instruction along the way to aid the child in building a generic code to use for all sorts of quantities. If we fail to do this, we say that the child has learned in rote fashion or that, in Wertheimer's (1945) moralistic way of putting it, we have given the child "mechanical" rather than "insightful" ways of solving the problem. The distinction is not between mechanical and insightful, really, but whether or not the child has grasped and can use the generic code we have set out to teach him.

You will sense immediately that what I have been describing are examples of "transfer of training," so-called. But nothing is being transferred, really. The organism is learning codes that have narrower or wider applicability.

Let me give you some examples of how one uses the transfer paradigm to investigate what kind of coding systems are being learned. William Hull, a teacher in a Cambridge school, raised the question whether the learning of spelling involved simply the learning by rote of specific words or whether instead it did not also involve learning the *general coding system* for English words from which the child might then be able to reconstruct the letters of a word. He took children of the fifth grade and separated them into those who had done well and those who had done poorly on a standard spelling achievement test, taking as subjects those who fell in the highest and lowest quartile of the class. He then presented these children brief exposures of pseudowords, which they were to write down immediately after the card bearing each word was removed. Some of the words were first-order approximations to English, essentially random strings of letters that had the same frequency distribution of letters as does English. Some were third- and fourth-order approximations to English constructed by Miller, Bruner, and Postman (1954) in connection with another experiment, words like MOSSIANT, VERNALIT, POKERSON, ONETICUL, APHYSTER, which reflected the probability structure of English very closely and which, but for the grace of God, might have been in the dictionary. Take the case for five-letter and six-letter pseudowords. For the first-order or random words, there was little difference between good and poor spellers. But for nonsense approximations to English, there was a great difference between the two, the good spellers showing a much superior performance.

The difference between the two groups is in *what* they had been learning while learning to spell English words. One group had been learning words more by rote, the others had been learning a general coding system based on the transitional probabilities that characterize letter sequences in English. Along the same lines, Mr. Robert Harcourt of Cambridge University and I used the occasion of an international seminar at Salzburg to test Italian, German, Swedish, French, Dutch, and English speakers on their ability to reproduce random strings of letters presented briefly (that is, zero-order approximations to any language), and third-order approximations to each of these languages. As you would expect, there was no difference in ability to handle random strings, but a real difference in ability, favoring one's mother tongue, in reproducing nonsense in one's own language. You will sense immediately to what language stock each of the following nonsense words belongs: MJÖLKKOR, KLOOK, GERLANCH, OTIVANCHE, TRIANODE, FATTO-LONI, and so on. When one learns a language one learns a coding system that goes beyond words. If Benjamin Lee Whorf is right, the coding system goes well beyond even such matters as we have described.

Let us sum up the matter to this point. We propose that when one goes beyond the information given, one does so by virtue of being able to place the present given in a more generic coding system and that one essentially "reads off" from the coding system additional information either on the basis of learned contingent probabilities or learned principles of relating material. Much of what has been called transfer of training can be fruitfully considered a case of applying learned coding systems to new events. Positive transfer represents a case where an appropriate coding system is applied to a new array of events, negative transfer being a case either of misapplication of a coding system to new events or of the absence of a coding system that may be applied. It follows from this that it is of the utmost importance in studying learning to understand systematically *what it is* that an organism has learned. This is the cognitive problem in learning.

There is perhaps one additional thing that is learned by an organism when he acquires information generically, and this must be mentioned in passing although it is not directly germane to our line of inquiry. Once a situation has been mastered, it would seem that the organism alters the way in which new situations are approached in search of information. A maze-wise rat, for example, even when put into a new learning situation, seems not to nose about quite so randomly. In an experiment by Goodnow and Pettigrew (1955), for example, once their subjects have learned one pattern of pay-off on a "two-armed bandit," they approach the task of finding other patterns by responding more systematically to the alternatives in the situation. Even when they are trying to discover a pattern in what is essentially a random series of pay-offs, their sequential choice behavior shows less haphazardness. It is interesting that this acquired regularity of response makes it possible for them to locate new regularities in pay-off pattern when these are introduced after a long exposure to random positional pay-offs. Even though the behavior is designed to discover whether the old pattern will recur again, its regularity makes it possible to discover new patterns.

Three general problems now emerge. The first problem concerns the conditions under which efficient and generalizable coding systems will be acquired. What will lead a rat to learn the sequence LRLR in such a generic way that it will be transferable to the sequence of turns RLRL? What will lead a child to learn the sequence 2, 4, 8, 16, 32 . . . in such a way that it transfers to the sequence 3, 9, 27, 81 . . . ? This we shall call *the conditions of code acquisition.*

The second we may label the *problem of creativity.* It has two aspects. The first has to do with the *inventive* activity involved in constructing highly generic and widely appropriate coding systems, armed with which a person will subsequently, in a highly predictive way, be able to deal with and go beyond much of the information he encounters in his environment. The other aspect of the problem of creativity is the development of a readiness to *utilize* appropriately already acquired coding systems. James long ago called this "the electric sense of analogy" and it consists in being able to recognize something before one fits it into or finds it to be a case of some more generic class of things that one has dealt with before — being able to see, for example, that laws that were originally related to statistical physics also fit the case of the analysis of transmitted information, the leap that carries us from Boltzmann's turn-of-the-century conception of entropy to modern theories of communication as initiated by Claude Shannon (1948). The equation of entropy with information was a creative analogical leap indeed, even if it did not require any new invention. Very well, the problem of creativity involves then the invention of efficient and applicable coding systems to apply to the information given and also the proper sense of knowing when it is appropriate to apply them.

The third and final problem to be considered is the *problem of instruction,* and it is a practical one. It concerns the best coding system in terms of which to present various subject matters so as to guarantee maximum ability to generalize. For example, the statement $S = \frac{1}{2} gt^2$ is an efficient and highly generalizable coding system for learning about falling bodies, and by using the code one can go beyond any partial data given one about falling bodies. But how does one teach somebody "about a country" in general so that given some new specific knowledge about the country he can effectively "go beyond it" by appropriate inferences based on an effective coding system?

We consider each of these problems in turn.

Conditions Affecting the Acquisition of Coding Systems

Essentially, we are asking under what conditions will an organism learn something or, as we put it, code something in a generic manner so as to maximize the transferability of the learning to new situations?

Let me propose four general sets of conditions that may be relevant here. The first of these is *set* or *attitude*. The second is *need state*. The third is *degree of mastery* of the original learning from which a more generic coding system must be derived. The fourth is *diversity of training*.

The role of set.   It is a perennial source of embarrassment to psychologists interested in the learning process that "set to learn" is such a massive source of variance in most experiments on human learning. We make the distinction between incidental learning and intentional learning. What is the difference between the two?

Take typical experiments in the field of concept attainment as a case in point. In most such experiments since Hull's classic study (1920), the subject is given the task of *memorizing* what nonsense syllables go with what figures or pictures or words. One subset of pictures in the array presented — ones that all contain unbeknownst to the subject a certain common defining property — will have the label CIV and another subset, let us say, will have the label DAX. The task as presented is one in which the subject is to learn which label goes with which pictures. Insofar as the task is understood as one involving the memorization of labels, the subject is engaged in what can only be called incidental concept attainment. An interesting experiment by Reed (1946) shows that when subjects operate under such a set, they attain concepts more slowly and remember them less well than under instructional conditions where the subject is told frankly what is the real objective of the experiment — that is, to find what makes certain designs CIV's and others DAX's. In an extensive series of experiments by Bruner, Goodnow, and Austin (1955), moreover, it is evident that the search for the defining attributes of a class of objects — the search for a generic code in terms of which a class of objects may be rendered equivalent — leads to certain forms of behavior strategies or learning sets that are absent when the task is seen as one of rote memorization. The subject learns ways of testing instances to gather an optimum amount of information leading him to final discovery of the defining attributes of CIV's and DAX's. Once success has been achieved in this way, new instances can be recognized with no further learning and the memory of the instances already encountered need no longer depend upon sheer retention. For now, knowing the code, the subject can reconstruct the fact that all positive instances encountered were all marked by certain critical attributes.

In short, an induced set can guide the person to proceed nongenerically and by rote or to proceed as if what was to be learned was a principle or a generic method of coding events. Instructions serve, if you will, as a switching mechanism or set producer that brings different forms of coding into play and tunes the organism to the kind and level of generic activity that seem appropriate to the situation.

Obviously, the principal giver of instruction is our own past history. For by virtue of living in a certain kind of professional or social setting, our approach to new experience becomes constrained — we develop, if you will, a professional deformation with respect to ways of coding events. The mathematician tends with time to code more and more events in terms of certain formal codes that are the stock in trade of his profession. The historian has his particular deformations, and so too the psychologist. With experience, Harlow's (1949) monkeys gradually develop a deformation too and attempt to solve all discrimination problems as exemplars of the oddity principle.

It is perhaps Kurt Goldstein (1939) who has insisted most strongly that one may in general characterize the typical sets a person brings to problems along the dimensions of abstractness and concreteness. The person who is high in concreteness deals with information or events in terms of their own specific identity and does not tend to genericize what is learned. The abstract attitude is one in which the individual can not only tear himself away from the given, but actually may not deal with the given save as an exemplar of more generic categories. How people "get to be" one way and the other or how they maintain an ability to operate at both levels is something we do not understand with any clarity, although some tentative proposals will be put forth in the following section.

To sum up: the manner and the degree with which newly learned knowledge is coded generically can be influenced in a transient way by situational instruction and in a more permanent way by the regimen of one's past experience. One's "attitude" toward learning, whether a transient or an enduring thing, will then determine the degree to which one is equipped with coding systems that can be brought to bear on new situations and permit one to go beyond them.

Need state. I should like to dust off the Yerkes-Dodson Law at this point and propose that the generality of the coding system in terms of which newly acquired information is organized depends upon the presence of an optimum motivational state. Very high and very low drive lead, I think, to an increase in concreteness of cognitive activity. There is a middle state of drive level that produces the strongest tendency toward generic learning.

Let me illustrate this by going back to the experiment of Bruner, Matter, and O'Dowd previously referred to. Consider two of their groups. Each group was given enough training to reach a criterion in learning the turn pattern LRLR and then given eighty additional trials of overlearning. The only difference between the groups was that one group did its learning under thirty-six hours of food deprivation, the other under twelve hours of deprivation. When the two groups were then transferred to the reversal pattern, RLRL, the moderately motivated group showed positive transfer, learning the new single alternation pattern significantly faster than they had learned the original pattern. The very hungry group showed marked negative transfer.

The behavior of the two groups at the time of transfer is revealing. When transferred, the moderately motivated groups showed much more disturbance in behavior. When these highly trained animals found the old reliable door at the first turn blocked, they drew back from the choice-point and sometimes took as long as twenty minutes before they could make up their minds about what to do next. They defecated, seemed upset, and spent a great deal of time looking back and forth at the two doors. Several of the animals, at the end of this period of delay, then charged through the now correct first door and continued to charge right through the now correct single alternation pattern and made no errors from then on. Others made somewhat more errors, but on the whole, their learning was rapid.

The other group, the highly skilled and highly motivated rats of the thirty-six-hour deprived group, showed quite different behavior. Finding the first door locked, they barged right over and took the alternative door, and then attempted unsuccessfully at each successive alley to make their old turn. Some of these animals persisted in this for many trials and then shifted to other forms of systematic response — such as one-sided position habits — that were not single alternation. In sum, it seemed as if they had to unlearn the old pattern of LRLR responses and then relearn a new one.

There is one particular feature of the behavior of the animals in the two groups that wants special attention. It is the amount of "looking around" or VTE-ing or scanning that went on in the two groups. As Tolman (1938) has observed, highly motivated organisms show less VTE behavior, less looking back and forth at choice points. So, too, our thirty-six-hour hungry animals during original learning in contrast with the twelve-hour ones. The difference in VTE was particularly marked during the early transfer trials as well, and it was exhibited by the less hungry rats predominantly in the first unit of the maze, at the choice-point that was the only real alternative, for once the first turn was correctly mastered, the rest of the pattern followed.

It would seem, then, that under conditions of high drive, if a path to the goal has been learned, it is learned, so to speak, as "*this* path to *this* goal" and is not coded or acquired as an example of a more generic pattern, "this *kind* of path to this *kind* of goal." In consequence, when a new situation arises, the driven creature does not have a generic coding system that permits him to go beyond it "insightfully." It is as if one of the students of geometry in Wertheimer's study (1945) had learned to do the operations necessary for solving the area of *this* parallelogram but had not generalized the knowledge into a coding system for handling parallelograms of slightly different size, shape, or position.

Impelling drive states seem also to affect the extent to which a person is able to apply already very firmly acquired coding systems to new material encountered, permitting him to go appropriately beyond the information given. An illustrative study is provided by the experiment of Postman and Bruner (1948) on perception under stress. Two groups of subjects were used. They began by having to recognize brief, three-word sentences presented tachistoscopically under usual laboratory conditions. Then the stress group was given an impossible perceptual recognition task to perform (reporting on the details of a complex picture presented at an exposure level too brief in duration for adequate performance). During these stress trials they were rather mercilessly badgered by the experimenter for performing so poorly and were urged to try harder. The other group was given a simple task of judging the illumination level at which the same picture was presented at the same exposure levels. And they were not badgered. Then additional sentences were given subjects in both groups. The stress group showed no further improvement in their sentence- and word-recognition thresholds, the nonstress group continued to improve. What was striking about the performance of the two groups in the latter half of the experiment was that the stress subjects either overshot the information given and made wild inferences about the nature of the briefly presented words, or they undershot and seemed unable to make words out of the briefly presented data at all. In terms of the Jamesian electric sense of analogy, it was as if the stress introduced either too many ohms of resistance into the circuit or removed too many of them. The stress subjects, let it be noted, did not behave consistently in the overshoot or the undershoot fashion, but seemed to go back and forth between the two.

Let me note finally in connection with code acquisition and/or the transfer of acquired codes to new situations that there is one interesting feature of the Harlow (1948) experiments on the acquisition of learning sets that is not often enough remarked. Recall that in the typical experiment of this kind, an animal is trained to choose the odd member of a set of stimuli, and that after training on a variety of such problems he is able to do so regardless of what characteristics the stimuli have: the odd one of several shapes, of several colors, of several junk stimuli, and so on. These experiments are carried out with animals who are only very lightly motivated. They are well fed before they are run, the reward used consists of a half or even a quarter of a peanut, and it would almost be fair to say that the most impelling drive operative is the manipulative-curiosity drive that Harlow has rightly made so much of in his recent writing. The use of such a mild motivational regimen is well advised. The fact of the matter is that one does not get such elegant principle learning in more highly motivated animals. A very hungry monkey may not develop such learning sets at all. Again, more generic coding seems to be inhibited by a condition in which the information to be acquired has too great instrumental relevance to a need state then in being.

Let me conclude this section on the role of need states in acquiring and utilizing coding systems with an important caveat, one that has been insisted upon particularly by George

Klein (1951). One cannot specify the cognitive or behavioral resultants of need states without specifying the manner in which the organism has learned to deal with his need states. The resultant of "learning to deal with needs" is the establishment in behavior of what Klein calls general regulatory systems. In a sense, we have been implying such systems in the rat and monkey when we speak of the fact that a high need state has the effect of specializing the organism to deal with the here-and-now without regard to the more generic significance of what is being learned. It is conceivable that in some higher organisms this may not always be the case.

Degree of mastery and its relationship to generic coding. Let me begin again with that overworked species, the rat. Starling Reed (1954) reports that animals who have been overtrained on a black-white discrimination, with black the positive stimulus, are able to transfer more easily to a black-white discrimination with white positive than are animals trained simply to criterion and then reversed. In the Bruner, Matter, and O'Dowd study already referred to, three groups of twelve-hour and three groups of thirty-six-hour hungry animals were used. High- and low-motivation groups were paired in terms of amount of original training given. One pair of groups was given original training on an LRLR pattern until they just reached criterion; a second pair was given twenty additional trials of practice beyond criterion; and the third pair was given eighty additional overtraining trials. The biggest effect in the study was in the interaction of drive level and amount of overtraining. For the twelve-hour groups, the more their overtraining, the better they did on transfer to the reverse pattern. But only the highly overtrained group showed positive transfer. All the strongly motivated animals showed about the same amount of negative transfer. We may take as a tentative conclusion that overtraining and mastery aids generic coding provided motivation is not severe.

We are in the midst of a controversial area, for the wisdom of common sense and of the psychologist divides sharply on the matter of practice and drill. "Practice makes perfect" is a well-thumbed proverb and the darling of practically all S-R learning theory. To be sure, it is a moot point in these theories just *what* it is that practice makes one perfect at. Nobody denies that it makes one perfect at the thing being practiced, but there is still debate on whether it also improves one at things beyond what one has practiced. The position of most stimulus-response theorists has been that it does not make one perfect at anything save the thing itself and that transfer to other things depends upon whether the other things contain elements identical to those that existed in the first task. We shall leave aside the question of how fast and loose one can play with the word "identical" in the expression "identical elements," for it is obvious that exploring its usage will be a discouraging venture. Even in the original monograph of Thorndike (1903) it was claimed that one form of identical element shared by two problems was that they could be solved by the same principle!

In any case, to return to the main issue at hand, there is another school of thought that proposed insight and understanding as a more important factor than drill in improving both performance of a particular task and in guaranteeing wider generalization of the learning to other situations. The names of Wertheimer (1945), Katona (1940), Duncker (1945), and Köhler (1925) are associated with this position, and the modern proverb has been provided by International Business Machines: THINK. The progressive school and its apostles have perhaps been the chief carriers of the practical banner.

I think the issue is a pseudoissue. The nature and effect of drill and overtraining is a function of what has to be learned. Moreover, one cannot speak of drill without specifying the nature of the set and the drive conditions under which it takes place. We cannot talk about practice or training as if it were being administered to an indifferently constructed black box.

First about the nature of materials to be learned. Take Katona's example of the string of numbers:

$$58121519222629$$

If subjects are asked to remember it, the amount of practice required to become perfect depends upon their method of recoding the numbers. If they recognize that the numbers are grouped as follows

$$5–8–12–15–19–22–26–29$$

and that this series begins with 5 and is made up of successive additions of 3 and 4, then what they had better practice is "5 then add 3 and then 4 and keep repeating this alternation." Mastering this coding system requires less practice and it is different practice than trying to remember the series by rote. As George Miller (1951) puts it in his delightful discussion of recoding systems, "Suppose that we want to know how far a body falls through space when it has been falling freely for a given number of seconds. One way to tackle this problem is to make measurements, summarize the measurements in a table, and then memorize the table . . . This is a very stupid way to proceed because we memorize each number as if it were unrelated to all the other numbers . . . All the measurements can be recoded into a simple rule that says the distance fallen at the end of t seconds is $gt^2/2$. The value of g is about 32. All we need remember is $16t^2$. Now we store all the measurements away in memory by storing this simple formula" (p. 234). Again, we had better practice remembering the formula and the value of g, and never mind practicing on the table of measurements from which it was produced.

But yet this fails to meet the question squarely. For where we do not know the appropriate coding system in advance, what is the best practice procedure for discovering it? Our rats and those of Starling Reed obviously had to do a fair amount of drilling at their task before they learned it in a generic way. And it seems to be frequently the case that a certain amount of skill development is necessary at a simpler level of coding before more generic recoding of the learning can occur. The earliest studies of code learning, the classic study by Bryan and Harter (1897) of telegraphic code learning, can be reproduced in many later studies: one first learns to code the messages in terms of letters, then in terms of words, then in terms of sentences. Later methods of regrouping or recoding depend upon prior mastery of less generic methods of coding. One's limited immediate memory span requires one to deal first with the dits and dahs of single letters. Then gradually when the dit-dah arrangement of a letter takes on unitary properties, that is, can be categorized as a unit, it may be grouped with other unitary dit-dah arrangements into words. When words are codable as units, then one goes to sentences. So too with the rats: they must master the regularity of a set of turns before it becomes possible to reorganize or recode in terms of a single alternation principle.

In sum, then, the question of mastery comes down to this. Learning often cannot be translated into a generic form until there has been enough mastery of the specifics of the situation to permit the discovery of lower-order regularities which can then be recombined into higher-order, more generic coding systems. Once a system of recoding has been worked out whereby information is condensed into more generic codes, the problem of mastery becomes one of mastering the recoding system rather than mastering the original set of events. Moreover, the nature of practice cannot be simply specified in terms of repetition to and beyond mastery of a specific task. Rather, one must specify the conditions under which practice takes place, whether with the auxiliary intention to search out a generic coding system or whether simply with a rote learning intention. Finally, the need level at which the organism is practicing a task must also be specified. Practice at a high rate of drive may produce no generic learning. Low-drive practice may.

Diversity of training. I think that we know intuitively that if we wish to make a group of students understand the Pythagorean theorem in plane geometry, it helps to illustrate the intuitive proof of the theorem to use several right triangles of different dimensions, and indeed it might also help to demonstrate that the theorem does not apply to nonrectilinear triangles. It also seems intuitively right, does it not, that if monkeys are to be taught Harlow's oddity problem it helps or indeed may be essential to give them training choosing the odd member of several *different* arrays? So too when we play the original word game with children, we point to several exemplars of the word "dog" and several exemplars of "cat" in demonstrating the linguistic code utterance "cats and dogs are different." The quantitative informational importance of diversity of instances in concept attainment has been dealt with elsewhere and I would only like to consider some of the common-sense implications of the matter here.

The process of finding out what is generic about a given situation so that one can then deal with similar situations later — know their solution without having to go through the tedious business of learning all over again — consists essentially of being able to isolate the defining properties of the class of events to which the present situation belongs. In a concept-formation experiment, for example, if a subject is trying to discover what makes certain cards "positive" and certain ones "negative," his task is to discover which of the discriminable attributes or which combination of discriminable attributes are present in the positive instances and absent in the negative ones. I think one can think of the matter of diversity in terms of the interesting old proverb, "The fish will be the last to discover water," as indeed man was very late in discovering the atmosphere. Unless one is exposed to some changes, genericizing does not seem to be stimulated. Kurt Lewin had a subtle point when he urged that the best way to understand the nature of a social process was to try to change it, for only in the face of changes in events does one begin to have the information necessary to abstract generic properties.

This suggests a rather simple but rather startling conclusion. If we are to study the conditions under which generic learning occurs, the pattern of much of present learning research needs drastic change. The present approach is to study the speed of acquisition of new learning and, possibly, to study the conditions that produce extinction. When we have carried our experimental subjects through these steps, we either dismiss them or, if they are animal subjects, dispose of them. The exception, of course, is the clinician, but even his research on learning and cognition is of the cross-sectional type. We have been accustomed to speaking of maze-wise rats and test-wise human beings, but in the spirit of being annoyed by an inconvenience.

The fact of the matter is, as Beach (1954) has recently pointed out, that early and diverse training of lower organisms seems to be one of the conditions for producing "intelligent" behavior in the more mature organism. If we really intend to study the conditions of generic learning by the use of the transfer-of-training paradigm I have proposed, then we shall have to keep our organisms far longer and teach them original tasks of greater diversity than we now do if we are to discover the conditions affecting generic learning.

The Invention or Creation of Coding Systems

The past half century has witnessed a profound revolution against the conception of science inherited from the Newtonian period. Newton saw the task of the scientist as a journey on the sea of discovery whose objective was to discover the islands of truth. The conception was essentially Baconian. Newton's *Principia* was not proposed as a theoretical system but as a description of discoveries about nature. His *Opticks* was in like vein a disquisition into the secrets of light. Indeed, Jonathan Edwards preached to his parishioners in Western Massachusetts on Newton's discovery of the spectral composition of white light as an instance of the fact that God had given man sufficient capacities to see through to some of the deepest secrets of God's design. To a considerable extent, the layman's view of science is still dominated by the spirit of discovery, by the spirit of naturalistic realism.

The temper of modern science is more nominalistic. The scientist constructs formal models or theories that have predictive value, that have a value in going beyond the information available. One works with sets of observations that one fits into a theory. If the theory cannot take one beyond one's observations, if it does not have the "surplus value" that is demanded of a theory, then the theory is trivial. The universe is a set of perspectives devised by scientists for understanding and rendering predictable the array of observations that are possible. Whoever has read Robert Oppenheimer's account of "Lord Rutherford's World" in his Rieth Lectures (1954) or whoever has read Max Wertheimer's account (1945) of his conversations with Einstein on the formulation of the special and general theories of relativity cannot but be struck by the emphasis on the constructive, nominalistic, and essentially subjective conception of science-making that prevails in modern physical theory.

The activity of constructing formal models and theoretical constructs is a prototype of what we mean by the creation of generic coding systems that permits one to "go beyond" the data to new and possibly fruitful predictions.

Let us consider the creative acts by which a person constructs a "theory" for dealing with a problem. The given, let us say, is as it is in a Duncker-type problem. Here is x-ray apparatus capable of destroying a tumor in the center of a body. The difficulty is that the amount of radiation sufficient to destroy the tumor is also sufficient to destroy the healthy tissue through which it must pass in reaching the tumor. How solve the difficulty? Let us assume that the problem solver did not learn a routine technique in medical school for dealing with this problem.

We will assume (and it is not an outrageous assumption, as we shall see) that the person has had experiences that provide the elements out of which a solution may be fashioned. The child knows, for example, that if a plank is too weak to take two children across a gap simultaneously, the children can get across one at a time in successive order or get across the gap at the same time if they can find two planks to throw across it. This is highly relevant knowledge. But this is not a "theory" nor by remembering it does one either solve the problem or create a relevant coding system.

Suppose now that the person comes, through whatever processes are involved, to a solution of the problem: using two x-ray beams, each of less than lethal dose, to converge at some angle upon the tumor. This solution, insofar as it is specific to the single problem at hand, is still not a theory; indeed it is not altogether clear that anything new has been "produced" or "created." What we mean by a theory or model or generic coding system is a representation of the criterial characteristics of the situation just described, a contentless depiction of the ideal case, empty in the sense that geometry is empty of particulars. It is this emptying operation, I would propose, that constitutes the creative step in inventing or producing a coding system. It is also the step that is involved when one learns something generically. In this sense there is only a difference in degree between what we have spoken of as generic learning and what we here call the production of a generic coding system.

Pursue the matter a bit further. The problem solver says to himself, "This must be a general characteristic of loads, media, and destinations within the medium. Every medium has an array of paths to a destination within it and each path has a capacity. The number of paths required for the simultaneous transmission of a load to a destination is the size of the load divided by the capacity of any single path." Now we say the person has a theory: he has to some degree emptied the problem of specific content.

When we ask what leads to such an emptying operation (or abstraction, if one prefers the more conventional term), we are forced to answer by describing the conditions that inhibit it. What then inhibits "theory construction"? I would submit that the conditions inhibiting theory construction of this kind are the same ones that inhibit generic learning — the conditions of code acquisition described in the preceding section. For generic learning and the abstracting or "emptying" operation are, I think, the same thing.

But consider one other aspect of the creation or acquisition of generic coding systems. It consists of a form of combining activity that is made possible by the use of abstracted or "empty" codes. Take the formulation just given — the theory of loads, media, destinations, and path capacities. It now becomes possible to combine *this* formalized system with other formalized systems to generate new predictions. For example, suppose the problem solver goes on to combine his new formulation with the equally abstract formulations of analytic geometry. The number of paths converging through a medium to an enclosed destination is infinity. Therefore, the combined path capacity of an over-all medium is infinity, and therefore, in principle, an infinite load (radiation or whatnot) can be delivered to a destination. In principle, then, one may go beyond to the hypothesis that *no* load is too large to deliver simultaneously across a medium, given the solution of technical limitations.

It seems to me that the principal creative activity over and beyond the construction of abstracted coding systems is the combination of different systems into new and more general systems that permit additional prediction. It is perhaps because of this that, in Whitehead's picturesque phrase, progress in science seems to occur on the margins between fields. There is virtually no research available on this type of combinatorial creativity. How, for example, do physiological psychologists combine the coding systems of biology and psychology, or biophysicists their component disciplines to derive a new emergent? We might begin by looking.

The Problem of Instruction

What we have said thus far obviously has implications for educational practice, and it is with one of these that we wish to conclude. How shall we teach a subject matter? If the subject matter were geometry we readily answer that we teach the person those axioms and theorems — a formal coding system — that will maximize the ability of the individual to go beyond the information given in any problem he might encounter. A problem in geometry is simply an incomplete statement, one that has unknowns in it. We say, "Here is a three-sided figure: one side measures x, and the other y, the angle between them is z degrees and the problem is to find the length of the other side and the size of the other two angles as well as the area of the triangle." One must, in short, go beyond what is given. We know intuitively that if the person has learned the formal coding system, he will be able to perform such feats.

But how describe the history of a people or, say, Navaho culture? I would propose that much the same criterion should prevail here as we apply to geometry. The best description of a people's history is that set of propositions that permits a given individual to go beyond the information given to him. This, if you will, is *"the"* history of a people, the information that is necessary to make all other information as redundant or predictable as possible. So too in characterizing Navaho culture: that minimum set of propositions that will permit the largest reconstruction of unknowns by people to whom the propositions are revealed.

Let me in general propose this test as a measure of the adequacy of any set of instructional propositions — that once they are grasped, they permit the maximum reconstruction of material unknown to the reconstructor. My colleague Morton White (1950) argues persuasively for this position when he says (pp. 718–719),

We ought to start by observing that a history contains true statements about the whole course of . . . [an] object's existence. True statements about the future of the object will be as much part of its history as true statements about its remote past. We must observe that some of these statements have causal implications whereas others do not . . . The next thing to observe is that there are two kinds of historians, two kinds of students who *want* to approximate the whole truth about a given object. First there are those who conceive it as their task to amass as many true singular statements as can be amassed at a given moment, and in this way approximate the ideal of the historian. Clearly this seems like the way to approach an infinite or very large number of statements — gather as many as you can. But then there are historians who are more discriminating, who recognize that some singular statements are historically more important than others, not because they fit in with some moral point of view, but because they are more useful for achieving the history of the object as here defined. The first group is near-sighted. It tries to amass everything in sight on the theory that this is a sure method of getting close to the whole truth. But it fails to realize that those who select facts which seem to have causal significance are more apt to come to know things about the future and past of the object.

White then goes on to compare the criterion of "causal fertility" in history with the criterion of "deductive fertility" in logic, noting that "both attempts at brevity . . . are motivated by a desire for intellectual economy." In the broadest sense, the economy is a predictive economy — to be able to go beyond givens to a prediction of unknowns.

I would submit, I think, that it is only by imparting "causally fertile" propositions or generic codes that general education in the broad range of human knowledge is made possible. General education does best to aim at being generic education, training men to be good guessers, stimulating the ability to go beyond the information given to probable reconstructions of other events.

Conclusion

This has been a programmatic essay on the conditions by which it becomes possible for people to go beyond the information given them, or as Bartlett (1951) has put it, to go beyond evidence, to fill in gaps, to extrapolate. We have posed the problem as one involving the learning of coding systems that have applicability beyond the situation in which they were learned. In essence, our proposal is that we emphasize those conditions that maximize the transferability of learning and in pursuit of that we have urged that psychologists examine more closely what is involved when we learn generically — the motivational conditions, the kinds of practice required, the nature of the set designed for gaining an optimally generic grasp of materials. Rate of acquisition and rate of extinction in learning have occupied us for a generation. Perhaps in the coming generation we can concern ourselves more directly with the utility of learning: whether, one thing having been learned, other things can be solved with no further learning required. When we have achieved this leap, we will have passed from the psychology of learning to the psychology of problem solving.

BIBLIOGRAPHY

1. Bartlett, F. C. Thinking. *Manchester Memoirs*, 93, No. 3 (The Clayton Memorial Lecture, 1951) (1951).
2. Beach, F. A., and J. .Jaynes. The effects of early experience on the behavior of animals. *Psychol. Bull.*, 51:239–263 (1954).

3. Bexton, W. H., W. Heron, and T. H. Scott. Effects of decreased variation in the sensory environment. *Canadian J. Psychol.*, 8: 70–76 (1954).

4. Bruner, J. S., J. J. Goodnow, and G. A. Austin. *A Study of Thinking.* New York: Wiley (1956).

5. Bryan, W. L. and N. Harter. Studies on the telegraphic language. The acquisition of a hierarchy of habits. *Psychol. Rev.*, 6:345–375 (1897).

6. Duncker, K. On problem solving. *Psychol. Monogr.*, 58:1–112 (1945).

7. Goldstein, K. *The Organism.* New York: American Book Co. (1939).

8. Goodnow, J. J., and T. Pettigrew. Responding to change and regularity in environmental events (in preparation). (1955).

9. Harlow, H. F. The formation of learning sets. *Psychol. Rev.*, 56:51–65 (1949).

10. Hull, C. L. Quantitative aspects of the evolution of concepts. *Psychol. Monogr.*, No. 123 (1920).

11. Humphrey, G. *Thinking.* New York: Wiley (1941).

12. James, W. *The Principles of Psychology.* New York: Holt (1890).

13. Katona, G. *Organizing and Memorizing.* New York: Columbia Univ. Press (1940).

14. Klein, G. S. "The personal world through perception," in R. R. Blake and G. V. Ramsey (eds.), *Perception: An Aproach to Personality.* New York: Ronald (1951).

15. Köhler, W. *The Mentality of Apes.* New York: Harcourt Brace (1925).

16. Miller, G. A. *Language and Communication.* New York: McGraw-Hill (1951).

17. Miller, G. A., J. S. Bruner, and L. Postman. Familiarity of letter sequences and tachistoscopic identification. *J. gen. Psychol.*, 50: 129–139 (1954).

18. Miller, G. A., G. A. Heise, and W. Lichten. The intelligibility of speech as a function of the context of the test materials. *J. exp. Psychol.*, 41:329–335 (1951).

19. Oppenheimer, J. R. *Science and the Common Understanding.* New York: Simon and Schuster (1954).

20. Piaget, J. *The Child's Conception of Physical Causality.* London: Kegan, Paul (1930).

21. Postman, L. and J. S. Bruner. Perception under stress. *Psychol. Rev.*, 55:314–323 (1948).

22. Reed, H. B. Factors influencing the learning and retention of concepts. I. The influence of set. *J. exp. Psychol.*, 36:71–87 (1946).

23. Reed, S. The development of noncontinuity behavior through continuity learning. *J. exp. Psychol.*, 46:107–112 (1953).

24. Shannon, C. E. A mathematical theory of communication. *Bell Syst. Tech. J.*, 27:379–423, 623–656 (1948). Also in C. E. Shannon

and W. Weaver, *The Mathematical Theory of Communication*, Urbana: Univ. of Illinois Press (1949).

25. Smith, S. Studies of recoding. Reported by G. A. Miller, The Magic Number 7 ± 2. Address given at the 1955 meetings of the Eastern Psychological Association, Philadelphia (1955).

26. Spearman, C. *The Nature of Intelligence and the Principles of Cognition*. London: Macmillan (1923).

27. Thorndike, E. L. *Educational Psychology*. New York: Lencke and Buechner (1903).

28. Tolman, E. C. The determiners of behavior at a choice point. *Psychol. Rev.*, 45:1–41 (1938).

29. Wertheimer, M. *Productive Thinking*. New York: Harper (1945).

30. White, M. G. "Toward an analytic philosophy of history," in M. Farber, *Philosophical Thought in France and the United States*, Buffalo: Univ. of Buffalo Press (1950).

31. Wilkins, M. C. The effect of changed material on ability to do formal syllogistic reasoning. *Arch. Psychol.*, No. 102 (1928).

DISCUSSION

Fritz Heider

THE first point I want to mention concerns the term "coding." We will hear it used again and again. I shall use Brunswik's paradigm: distal stimulus — proximal stimulus — intraorganismic events — proximal reactions — distal effects. Now, when Bruner talks about coding, I think he means that either proximal or distal stimuli are encoded in terms of some systems of coding, which in this diagram we will have to consider as intraorganismic events or structures. In order to make sense of the environment or in order to get into contact with the environment, we have to assimilate it in some way or we have to transform it into our own terms. That, I take it, is what Bruner means by coding. We shall see that Osgood regards that as the decoding process — he would call "encoding" the portion stretching from the central processes to the responses. And Brunswik, in his paper, used the term "encoding" when he talked about the relation between distal stimulus and proximal stimulus, and the term "decoding" he applied to the process of utilizing proximal stimuli in perception. Well, it seems to me that when we use the terms "coding" and "decoding," we always talk about a translation, so to speak, from one language into another language, or from one system of representation into another system. And when we talk about decoding, we forget the language into which we translate; we are only concerned with the language from which we translate. When we talk about encoding we are mainly concerned with the language into which we translate. But in every case of translation from one language into another, or from one system of manifolds into another system, there is both encoding and decoding. That is how, I think, one can make a bridge between Bruner's "coding" and the "decoding" about which we will hear later.

The second point concerns the equivalence categories. You remember that there are two points here, illustrated by two examples, of how one goes beyond the information given. The one is the equivalence category, which allows us to go beyond sense data to the class identity. I think you remember the example with the apple. And the second point is the redundancy of the environment with the example of reading a word with letters missing. I cannot help wondering why there are these two groups — whether the first one is not also a redundancy.

The next point refers to something similar, to the relation between formal and empirical components, or systematic and empirical components, in this encoding. To learn probabilities would mean to learn low-order empirical laws. And then, the formulation of relationships between acceleration and some other variables, for instance, implies a fitting of a systematic network of concepts to an empirical manifold. Now, Bruner rightly remarked that in some cases we use partly this probabilistic learning of low-order empirical relations, partly the higher or more formal order of learning. That is one possibility: that the two can be used at the same time side by side in order to solve the same problem. But there is also another possibility, which he mentioned in his paper at a later point, namely, that the encoding into a formal coding system helps us in collecting experiences. In many cases, when we learn these probabilistic connections, we learn them only because we have a formal system that gives us the concepts and allows us to see the regularities. That is in a way illustrated by the experiment of Goodnow and Pettigrew, which Bruner mentioned: after learning one pattern, subjects respond more systematically to the alternatives in the situation. That is the role of theory in acquiring facts. Piaget, for instance, has some beautiful examples. He says that children do not recognize that the level of water is horizontal in a tipped glass because to be able to see that it is horizontal they need some reference to a more abstract space. Only when they have that, can they have the experience that the level stays the same in spite of tipping. Bruner mentioned common-sense ideas as an example of low-order empirical learning; I would say that even in common sense we have certain formal systems. During the last years I have been trying to find out more about the system of common-sense psychology, its concepts, and how they are related. Underlying our ordinary common-sense language in which we talk about other people and in which we talk about interpersonal relations is a structure of concepts that is, in some cases, rather exact and like any scientific structure of systematic concepts. So I would say that our common-sense view of the world is not based exclusively on low-order empirical connections and correlations.

Now, in regard to the conditions of code acquisition about which Bruner made some very interesting remarks: I wonder why he did not include in these conditions one which, judging from other parts of the paper, one would think he could have included — the factor of the stimulus pattern. A certain arrangement of stimuli, of cues, can help us very much in perceiving the general meaning of an event or a structure. In some cases it is very hard to see this general meaning. We don't see anything beyond the superficial layer — the skin, so to speak. In other cases we seem to see right through to deeper layers, and I think it is not chance that the movements of the planets or the free fall were the points where a more rigidly systematic physics started. These are the points where the laws of gravity show through on the surface. It is as if some of the skeleton of nature were exposed at certain points where we can have access to the underlying generalities more or less directly. In psychology, the subject matter is structured in such a way that the generalities are very deep, buried in the ground, so that some people merely give up digging and say, "Let's stay on the ground." I think the role of the stimulus pattern is recognized in the last section of the paper, the section on instruction. How do we teach people to see generalities? We prepare the material in such a way that the general structure becomes more visible, and that, after all, is also the secret of good style, and the secret of making a good table summarizing experimental results. One can make it in very different ways, as you all know; it can be made in such a way that one doesn't know at all what it is all about, and one can, just by rearranging it, make the general trends suddenly visible.

I want to mention one more point in regard to the learning of generic coding systems. Bruner seems to think that learning always proceeds from a specific to a generic form. First the lower-order regularities are discovered, then they are combined into higher and higher orders. I wonder whether there are not exceptions to this development. I wonder whether, in many cases, when one is used to handling material on low levels without generality, one doesn't often become settled and whether that may not really hinder one from seeing the general meanings. Very often amateurs in science or engineering are the ones who have the creative ideas and see through to the generic level because they do not have too much mastery of the material on a lower level. They have not learned anything that might hinder them from going further.

A BEHAVIORISTIC ANALYSIS
OF PERCEPTION AND LANGUAGE
AS COGNITIVE PHENOMENA

Charles E. Osgood
University of Illinois

Psychologists, when they are behaving like psychologists, limit themselves to observing what goes into the organism (stimuli) and what comes out (responses). Between these two observation points lies a Great Unknown, the nervous system. Nowadays it is fashionable to refer to this region as "a little black box." In any case, psychological theory, as distinct from psychological observation, is made up of hunches about what goes on in this little black box. Theories of hearing and color vision, principles of association, generalization, and reinforcement, notions about cohesive forces between like processes in a visual field — all imply certain conceptions about how the nervous system works. If these conceptions are made explicit, as Hebb (8) has done, for example, one is said to "neurologize," but, explicit or not, psychological theories select from among neurophysiological alternatives.

Behavior theories are often divided into two general classes — the S-S and S-R models. Each of these models is insufficient, an incomplete theory. The S-S model may adequately handle relations among input events and between these and central, "meaningful" events, but it says little or nothing about how they eventuate in behavior. For example, we are not told by Köhler (13) how a pattern of direct currents in the visual brain elicits those responses in vocal muscles which constitute saying "circle" or "square." Similarly, the S-R model may adequately handle rather simple relations between stimulus and response variables, but it says little or nothing about either the integration of sensory events (perception) or the integration of response events (motor skill). And neither model has had much to contribute to an understanding of symbolic processes.

Language is challenging to the behavior theorist because it includes at once the most complex organizations of perceptual and motor skills and the most abstract, symbolic processes of which the human animal is capable. It is also a necessary first step in the application of psychological principles to social behavior, because it is mainly via language that one nervous system establishes relationship with others. Perception presents equally difficult problems. Phenomena that have been called perceptual range the gamut from projection-system dynamics to meaningful processes, and certainly the integrational character of perception, which Gestalt psychologists have stressed, has been the Waterloo of contemporary behaviorism — I know of no S-R model that gives a convincing interpretation of standard perceptual phenomena. It is my hope that a combined analysis of language and perception may shed some light on both.

In the body of this paper I shall describe a highly speculative conception of behavior, which at least pretends to be a complete theory, in scope although certainly not in detail. It will necessarily imply a conception of how the nervous system operates — how it determines the relations we observe between stimulus inputs and response outputs — but I shall try to phrase the theory itself in psychological terms. It is a model that has gradually developed in the course of my work on language behavior. It envisages two stages and three levels of organization between stimulus and response in the complete behavioral act. The first stage is what I shall call *decoding,* the total process whereby physical energies in the environment are interpreted by an organism. The second stage is what I shall call *encoding,* the total process whereby intentions of an organism are expressed and hence turned again into environmental events. The three levels of organization are assumed to apply to both sides of the behavioral equation, to both decoding and encoding: (1) a *projection level* of organization, which relates both receptor and muscle events to the brain via "wire-in" neural mechanism; (2) an *integration level*, which organizes and sequences both incoming and outgoing neural events; and (3) a *representation* or *cognitive level*, which is at once the termination of decoding operations and the initiation of encoding operations. We have evidence for all three of these levels, but the principles that apply most parsimoniously to one do not apply easily to the others.

Projection

The receptor surface of the organism is rather precisely mapped upon the sensory cortex. Similarly, the voluntary muscle system is rather precisely mapped upon the motor cortex. The most direct evidence for these statements is the predictability of experienced sensations or muscle contractions when the sensory or motor cortex is explored electrically. One general principle of the projection level, then, is *isomorphism*. This does not mean that the projection level is simply an uncomplicated relay system. At the successive synaptic junctures between periphery and cortex transverse connections make possible lateral interactions of limited scope and kind. For example, across any band of impulse-bearing fibers at any synaptic level there seems to be in operation a principle of lateral facilitation and inhibition — more rapidly firing elements in the band are further facilitated by summation with impulses received laterally from more slowly firing elements, and conversely the firing of the slower elements is relatively damped by receiving laterally a more rapid, subthreshold barrage. Something of this sort seems to underlie sharpening of contours and segregation of figure from ground in vision, as well as the phenomenon of masking in audition.

One can also, I think, handle the major characteristics of both color and brightness contrast, such phenomena as the apparent solidity of objects viewed binocularly, the continuity of optimum visual movement, and figural after-effects with projection level mechanisms. This argument has been given in more detail in my book (23) and in the paper by Heyer and myself (24), which proposed an interpretation of figural after-effects alternative to that offered by Köhler and Wallach (13). It relies heavily on the work of Marshall and Talbot (16) and others on the functioning of the projection system.

The main point here is that there are many so-called perceptual phenomena that will probably be shown to depend upon projection mechanisms and hence be entirely predictable from knowledge of the stimulus and knowledge of projection dynamics. Such phenomena represent changes in the sensory signal itself, as I have defined it, rather than subsequent utilization of it in interaction with other signals.

Another characteristic of the projection level is that *its functioning is not modifiable by experience*. I know of no evidence showing that "what leads to what" in either sensory or motor projection systems can be modified by learning. The projection system is a perpetual *tabula rasa* — a centrally fixated object produces the same activity in Area 17 at twenty years as it did at twenty months, even though the subsequent utilization of these signals may be quite different. The experiments of Sperry (30) and others, in which segments of either sensory or motor projection systems are transplanted in embryo, also provide impressive evidence for the absence of functional modifications at this level — an animal operated upon in this manner will continue to lift the left limb when the right limb is shocked, for example, with no evidence of learning. Appropriately, the work of Senden (29), with human adults recovering sight for the first time, and Riesen (27), with chimpanzees reared in darkness, shows that certain so-called perceptual functions are independent of experience — primitive isolation of figure from ground, fixation of an object in space, contour formation, color and brightness differentiation, and certain others.

The salient point for the behavior theorist is this: because the projection systems do display these two characteristics — isomorphism and inability to modify through experience — we can depend on stimulus-and-response observations as faithful indices of the sensory and motor signals with whose more central interactions I think our science of behavior is concerned.

Integration

Even the crudest observations of behavior reveal that certain patterns and sequences of responses are more readily executed than others and that certain patterns and sequences of stimuli have priority over others. Apparently both motor and sensory signals are capable of becoming structured or organized. I think there is a very simple property of nervous tissues that accounts for such structuring, and D. O. Hebb (8) has already put his finger on it. *Whenever central neural correlates of projection-level signals are simultaneously active and in fibrous contact, either directly or mediately, an increased dependence of one upon the other results.* A few explanatory comments are in order about this statement. First, we must say that it is the more central neural correlates, rather than the sensory or motor signals themselves, which can thus be associated, because the projection systems are not modifiable through experience, as we have seen. There is no requirement that the central correlates of signals be isomorphic with these signals; in fact, existing evidence indicates that strict isomorphism breaks down beyond the sensory projection level. Secondly, strict simultaneity among the signals whose more central correlates are to be associated is not necessary; the work of Lorente de No and others describes reverberatory circuits which would prolong activation and hence make possible integration over time.

In a greatly oversimplified way, Figure I attempts to illustrate what I have in mind here. The isomorphic relations between stimuli and sensory signals and between responses and motor signals are shown on lower left and lower right respectively. It is assumed that cells at the termination of the projection system (for example, sensory or motor signals, as I have called them) have ample synaptic contacts with certain more central cells to guarantee exciting them (in the case of sensory decoding) or being excited by them (in the case of motor encoding). These are the cells in the integration level, *a, b,* and *c,* which I call "central correlates." This utilizes what I believe is a general principle of central nervous tissue: the probability of an antecedent neurone being a sufficient condition for the firing of a subsequent neurone is some direct function of the density of fibrous contact at their synapse. The control exercised by one cell over the firing of another may be increased, of course, by determining bombardment via mediate, circuitous routes; this is illustrated by cell *x* in the sensory integration system.

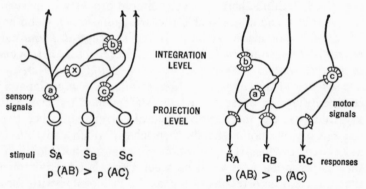

Figure 1

The conditions given in this diagram are such that *in the stimulus input* to this organism the contingency of events *A* and *B* is greater than that between events *A* and *C,* and similarly for responses *A* and *B* versus *A* and *C.* This means that the resultant tendency for central correlate *a* to activate central correlate *b* should be greater than its tendency to activate *c.* I have indicated this in the diagram by a thicker band of contacts on cell *b* from *a* than on cell *c* from *a.*

Now, as I said before, I wish to outline a psychological theory, not a neurological one. What kind of psychological principle seems to be embodied here? Given isomorphism between observables and signals, which makes it possible for me to deal directly with observable stimuli and responses, I can phrase the following pair of principles: *sensory integration — the greater the frequency with which stimulus events* A *and* B *are associated in the input to an organism, the greater will be the tendency for the central correlates of one,* a, *to activate the central correlates of the other,* b. This principle says in effect that patternings, regularities, and orderings of events in the stimulating environment of an organism come to be mirrored in the structuring of its sensory nervous system. *Motor integration — the greater the frequency with which response events* A *and* B *are associated in the output of an organism, the greater will be the tendency for the central correlates of one,* a, *to activate the central correlates of the other,* b. This says in effect that patternings, regularities, and orderings of the overt behavior of an organism, no matter how established, will come to be paralleled by equivalent organizations within its motor nervous system.

It should be stressed that what I am calling sensory and motor integrations function as classes of intervening variables, anchored directly to antecedent and subsequent observables, respectively, via a simple frequency-of-co-occurrence function. How would varying this frequency factor be expected to affect what is observed?

I suggest that *with high frequency of stimulus or response pairing the central correlates of one will become a sufficient condition for the excitation of the correlates of the other.* I shall call this an *evocative relation.* Behaviorally it means that the occurrence of some of a set of related stimulus events will produce the central experience of the others as well and be reported or responded to as such, without their external correlates necessarily being given at all; it means that the initiation of some elements of a response pattern will set the whole pattern going. *With a lower frequency of stimulus or response pairing, the central correlates of one will become merely a condition for "tuning up" the correlates of the other.* I shall call this a *predictive relation.* Perhaps here the energies delivered from the antecedent cell to the dependent cell, while not adequate to fire that cell, are available for summation with energies being delivered via the direct path. Behaviorally this would mean an experience-determined increase in the *stability* of both decoding and encoding processes by the organism — perception of certain cues would increase the probability of also perceiving others, in competition with many simultaneous stimuli; initiating certain responses would increase the probability of also initiating others, again in competition with many simultaneous action tendencies. In a sense we would have here a mechanism for reducing the "noise" in both decoding and encoding.

Let us look into some of the behavioral implications of this principle. In ordinary perceiving we seldom receive complete information — the environment is inspected with rapid, flighty samplings, and intensity-duration factors in the projection system certainly imply that these samplings must yield only partial signals — nevertheless, perceptual experiences are usually wholistic. I assume that what I have called *evocative relations*, based on high frequencies of input pairing or redundancy, underlie the well-documented closure and "filling in" phenomena. Directly relevant are some recent papers by Fred Attneave (1) in which he demonstrates that "various Gestalt-factors including symmetry, good continuation, and other forms of regularity may all be considered to constitute redundancy in visual stimulation and be quantified accordingly within a framework of information theory." I have not attempted myself the application of information-theory statistics to the phenomena subsumed under this integration principle, but I suspect they would be quite appropriate. We refer to "closure" when actual stimulus events, as independently measured, correspond to what is perceived, but the same tendency toward completion of an integrational unit lies at the base of many perceptual illusions, where the actual stimulus events do *not* correspond to what is integrated. I have an electric clock at home which can't be reset after the current has gone off briefly; I have to stop it and wait a day until time catches up. Every once in a while I glance up to find the time, and momentarily I see the sweep-second hand moving! Considering the thousands of times clock-face signals have been followed in my experience by sweeping second-hand signals, this illusion becomes understandable.

Merely *predictive relations* in perceptual decoding are also familiar in everyday experience. It is easier to follow a familiar juke-box tune than an unfamiliar tune against the uproar in a local tavern; the more familiar the camouflaged object in a complex picture, the more readily its contour can be traced. On the experimental side, I would interpret the findings of Bruner and Postman on the perception of incongruity (4) along these lines — the most common response to trick cards, say a *black* six of hearts, presented tachistoscopically, was to complete the integration set in motion by either the color *or* the form, but, as would be expected from the lack of reciprocal "tuning up," exposure times for decoding trick cards were significantly longer than for normal cards. Similarly, Hake and Hyman (7) have found that subjects will come to reflect in their predictions about successive stimuli the sequential dependencies built into the series, even though they may be unaware that these dependencies exist. Hake says (6), "It appears that the mechanism by which we develop expectancies about the occurrence of probabilistic events operates such that over longer series of trials or choice points we [come to] expect events about as often as they appear."

Turning now to integrations in *ordinary motor encoding,* it may be noted first that S–R behaviorists have always relied upon proprioceptive feedback as the mechanism for organizing motor skills — and this despite the fact that as long ago as 1917 Lashley pointed out that there simply wasn't enough time in rapidly executed skills for impulses to be carried to and from the sequentially activated muscle groups. In a more recent and very stimulating paper given in the Hixon Symposium (14), he makes this point again (p. 123): "Sensory control of movement seems to be ruled out in such acts. They require the postulation of some central nervous mechanism which fires with predetermined intensity and duration or activates different muscles in predetermined order. The mechanism might be represented by a chain of effector neurons, linked together by internuncials to produce successive delays in firing." This does not mean that proprioceptive feedback mechanisms are unimportant. On the contrary, I think that three stages in skill formation could be traced: (1) a very slow and uncertain patterning or ordering of responses on the basis of exteroceptive controls, as in imitating the seen movements of another person; this makes possible (2) a transfer gradually to proprioceptive controls (feedback), accompanied by considerably increased speed of execution; and this more rapid and stable organization in turn makes possible (3) a transfer to central programming in the integrational motor system which we are discussing.

Here again, a very high frequency of pairing should result in the formation of *evocative relations* among motor events. I call such tightly integrated patterns motor skill components." All the complex acts with which we deal as psychologists seem to be compounded of such components — "opening the door," for example, is a complex act involving an arm-extending-and-hand-opening component, a hand-closing component, a wrist-twisting component, and an arm-flexing component. These same elements, just like the syllables of spoken language, enter in various combinations into the myriad activities of everyday life. Motor integrations may lead to errors of completion analogous to perceptual illusions — in typing, my favorite error is regularly to add an "n" to the word *ratio*, presumably because of the tendency to complete the very common "ion" that terminates words like *action, fashion,* and of course, *ration*. Based on lower orders of frequency, many response-response integrations become merely *predictive motor relations* — unbuttoning one's shirt is predictive of peeling it off, lighting one's cigarette is predictive of blowing out the match (much to my occasional embarrassment when someone just then indicates the need of a light!) I do not mean that stimulus controls are absent in such predictive motor sequences; rather, the motor preparation decreases the probability of disturbance through ordinary stimulus changes. In other words, there seems to be a syntax of behavior just as there is a syntax of language, and this provides a stability of customary action that frees it from constant voluntary supervision.

The integrative mechanisms we have been discussing appear even more clearly in *language behavior,* and this is because the units of both decoding and encoding have been more sharply etched by linguists than have the units of nonlanguage behavior by psychologists. Generally speaking, we find evocative integrations in the smallest skill units of both speaking and listening, and predictive integrations in the grammatical mechanisms that interrelate larger message events.

The minimal units in language decoding are called *phonemes*. These are classes of similar sounds having a common significance in the code — for example, the initial sounds in "key" and "cool" are both members of the "k" phoneme, and their differences in auditory quality are entirely predictable from the message environment, in this case the following vowel. There are only some 32 phonemes in the English code; in other words, on the basis of amazingly high frequency of occurrence we have developed about 32 evocative auditory integrations, each one of which is set in motion by a *class* of input signals that varies in the elements actually present in any instance. Testimony to the general validity of our principle is the fact that ordinarily we are incapable of perceiving the differing members of these phoneme classes — *allophones,* as they are called. Only by adopting the analytic attitude of the linguist, which means listening to our language as sounds rather than meanings, can most of us hear the differences between the allophones of, say, the "p" in "pin," "spin," and "nip," in the allophones of "t" in "I boug*ht* a bi*tt*er bo*tt*le," yet these auditory distinctions are in themselves sufficient for speakers of other languages to arrange separate phoneme categories upon them. It is also interesting in this connection that our decoding of phonemes is on an all-or-nothing basis — when I say "he was a *trader,*" some of you heard "traitor" (to his country) and others heard "trader" (on the stockmarket), but none of you heard both at once or any compromise between the "t" and "d" phonemes. In other words, evocative integrations function as all-or-nothing units.

In language encoding, the smallest functional units are probably *syllables*. This is at least suggested by the work of Grant Fairbanks on delayed auditory feedback (6), in which he finds the interval of maximum interference to correspond to the rate of syllable production in ordinary speech (about 4/sec.); it is also suggested by the fact that slowing down one's speech is usually accomplished by prolongation of syllabic boundaries, for example, "syll-a-ble pro-duct-ion." Here again we have a limited number — much larger than the number of phonemes, to be sure — of motor patterns and sequences used with such high frequency that they become evocative integrations. Think of the number of word units in which the syllable "bit" appears — the word "bit" itself, "habit," "arbitrary," "bitter," "prohibit," "bitsy," and so on. These syllables involve both simultaneous and sequential integrations of many motor elements in the vocal system, and they come to function as units in behavior.

The operation of *predictive integrations* in language has a number of excellent experimental demonstrations. Postman, Bruner, and Walk (26), for example, have shown that imbedding a single reverse-printed letter in a meaningful word lengthens the tachistoscopic exposure time at which that letter can be reported *as* reversed more than imbedding it in a series of unrelated consonants — the normal configuration of the familiar word is thus highly predictive of its components — and this was true despite the fact that the average exposure time for letters in meaningful words was very much shorter than for letters in nonsense sequences, which also follows from the integration hypothesis. An experiment by Miller, Postman, and Bruner (18) shows that varying the sequential probabilities of orthographic materials affects their recognition times in the expected way. And we may add Shannon's finding that the guesses of subjects as to what letters should follow sequences of varying length matched very closely redundancy measurements made on large samples of English texts.

But it is in the *grammar* of a language that one observes the most remarkable predictions over time — a phenomenon which, interestingly enough, Lashley, in the Hixon Symposium mentioned earlier, took as his jumping-off point for an analysis of serial order in behavior. While in the rapidly flowing tide of conversation, both speakers and listeners attend to the lexical units in messages that represent semantic choices, leaving the complex grammatical and syntactical regularities to take care of themselves. It would be safe to say that the lay user of a language is almost never aware of its grammatical structure, couldn't possibly describe its laws, and yet follows them faithfully. When analyzed linguistically, the rules of grammar prove to be elaborate cases of redundancy or predictiveness. One such grammatical redundancy mechanism is *congruence:* in the present tense in English, the occurrence of a singular subject sets up a readiness for a verb ending in *s* (The boy run*s* but the boy*s* run); a time marker sets up a readiness for the appropriate tense tag on the verb (*Yesterday* in the city I *bought* a hat); a dependent clause marker sets up a readiness for the major clause (*When* I come, *open the door*). In terms of our model, it is the frequency with which such grammatical redundancies have been heard and produced that sets up in the nervous system predictive integrations that match the structure of the language. As would be expected, the longer the interval between congruent elements, the weaker becomes the set and the more likely errors.

Being a relatively uninflected language, English depends heavily upon syntactical *ordering* mechanisms, another grammatical redundancy. "John loves Mary" is quite a different proposition from "Mary loves John," as many a jilted lover has discovered. In Latin these words could be kept in the same order and the difference in implication borne by inflectional endings. If I say "the happy, little ———," all of you feel a strong tendency to fill in *some* noun. If I say "the farmer killed the ———," you have essentially two structural alternatives, a noun or a noun phrase (for example, *duck* or *ugly duckling*). If I say "the old man eats ———," the set of structural alternatives is larger, but still limited (a noun, *dinner, meat;* an adverb, *swiftly, heartily;* a prepositional phrase, *with his hands, on the table,* and so on). At each point in a language message, then, we have a hierarchy of structural alternatives, this hierarchy varying in its probabilistic character with the grammatical restrictions in the language as a whole. The closer the language user's nervous system can come to matching these restrictions with its own predictive integrations, the smoother become both decoding and encoding processes and the fewer decisions have to be handled by the semantic system.

By way of evidence that these grammatical redundancies do facilitate decoding and encoding, we might cite the following: Wilson Taylor (31), using his "cloz" procedure in which the subject fills in the gaps in mutilated messages, finds that with both sides of the gap given as in his method structural determinism is almost perfect (for example, in filling in "the old man ——— along the road," all subjects will fill in a verb form even though they vary semantically in what verb they choose). Miller and Selfridge (19) and others have demonstrated that ease of learning and retention of meaningful materials varies with the degree of approximation to English structure. Along similar lines, one of my students, Mr. Albert Swanson, compared the ease of learning nonsense sequences that retained the structure of the English sentences from which they were derived, for example,

The maff vlems oothly um the glox nerfs

with matched materials in which the grammatical cues had been eliminated, for example,

maff vlem ooth um glox nerf.

Despite the greater absolute amount of material in the structured forms, they were learned significantly more easily than the matched strings of nonsense items.

Before leaving this integrational level, we should deal at least briefly with a problem raised by the existence of these *hierarchies of alternatives*. In grammatical ordering mechanisms we have seen that at each choice-point in a message the speaker or hearer has available a set of alternative constructions, having different probabilities attached to them; similarly in perceptual decoding a particular subset of signals will be predictive of a hierarchy of potential integrations, each having a different probability associated with it. Take as examples the two sets of letters shown in Figure 2. Based on the absolute frequencies of occurrence in this type-face, integrations associated with O, C, Q, and G will have varying conditional probabilities upon occurrence of the subset of signals from the lefthand, which are common to all; their *absolute frequencies* of occurrence, however, are all probably sufficient to produce

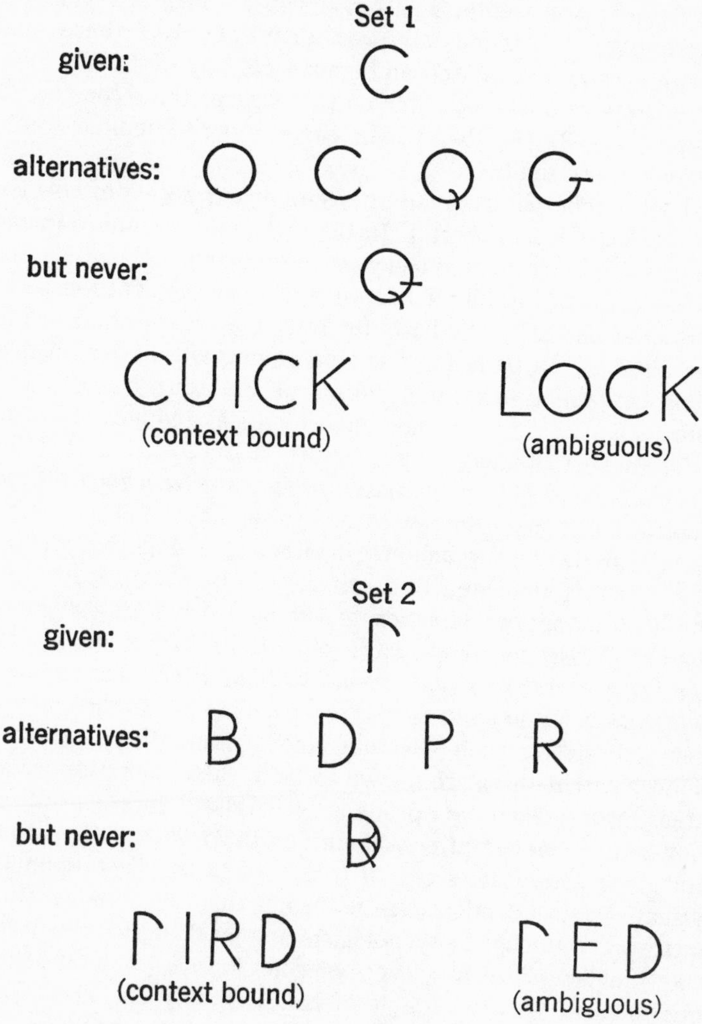

Figure 2

what I have called evocative integrations. Yet, given the arc as a stimulus set in the tachistoscope, one never sees all of these possibilities at once — perception would be a perpetual jumble if such were the case! Rather, we experience one alternative or another, that having the highest over-all momentary conditional probability. The larger context may select among alternatives — C is the only possibility in QUICK, but C and O are competitive in the ambiguous context of LOCK. The same arguments can be made on the basis of the second set of letters — B, D, P, R — where the composite jumble would be even more unlikely.

These facts require some extension of our notion of how the integrational level operates. In the first place, I think we must distinguish between frequency of co-occurrence of signals and redundancy within hierarchies of alternative integrations. The former seems to be the basis for setting up integrations, while the latter is the basis for selection among alternative integrations containing the same subset of initiating signals. Two integration hierarchies may have identical redundancy characteristics (for example, a .50, .30, .10, .05, .05 probability structure) and yet on the basis of absolute frequencies of occurrence one may be evocative throughout and the other merely predictive throughout; in either case, only that alternative which is momentarily dominant will be effective. And this implies this notion: *selection of the momentarily most probable integration among the hierarchy of alternatives based upon the same subset of signals serves to inhibit all other potential integrations*. I am not going to speculate upon the possible neural basis for such selection among alternatives, except to point out that there are known to be in the cortex "suppressor areas" whose excitation produces generalized spread of inhibition and Ruch tentatively identifies them with "attentional" functions (Area 19 seems to exert such an effect upon the visual system). I might also point out that many thoughtfully introspective people, psychologists among them, have reported the "singleness" of awareness or consciousness — as if at any one moment we are capable of handling only one item of information, the apparent multiplicity of attention being in reality a rapid succession. The integrational system seems to operate in such a way that many are called but only one is chosen.

Representation

Let's take a moment to see what kind of organism we've constructed so far. On the input side it is capable of rather faithfully recording as signals what events take place on its receptor surface; it is also able, on the basis of experience, to integrate these motor signals into evocative and predictive units that reflect redundancies in its own past behavior. But something is obviously missing: this organism does not connect with its own activities events that are happening in the world; it is completely "mindless" in the colloquial sense. In other words, we have so far dealt exclusively with S-S and with R-R relations, and what is missing are S-R relations.

Stimulus events may be related to response events at all levels of organization, and these associations may be either innate or acquired. Some sensory signals have an innate "wired-in" connection with specific responses (unconditioned reflexes) and additional classes of signals may acquire such direct connection with motor signals (conditioned reflexes). Similarly, at the integrational level, associations between complex patterns of sensory and motor signals may be innate — certainly, the complicated organization of instinctual sex behavior falls in this rubric, as does the "freezing" reaction of baby birds to certain complex retinal patterns. It also seems to be a general characteristic of the central nervous system that S-R relations *originally* organized on the "voluntary" level will, if repeated sufficiently often, become autonomous integrations — most sensory-motor skills seem to suffer this fate, reading aloud and typing as well as tying one's shoes and brushing one's teeth.

But the most important mechanism for associating sensory events with motor events — certainly in the human, and I suspect in the higher vertebrates in general — is via a *two-stage mediation process*. The essential notion here is that in the course of associating external stimuli with overt behavior some representation of this overt behavior becomes anticipatory, producing self-stimulation that has a symbolic function. There is nothing highly original about postulating such mediation processes. My own use of the notion stems directly from Hull's conception of the "pure-stimulus-act," which incidentally he suggested (11) would prove to be the basis of abstraction and symbolism in behavior; the same idea is used by Guthrie as "movement-produced-stimuli," and Tolman's basic conception of a "sign-significate-expectation" can, I think, be shown to be functionally identical. But whereas Hull and Guthrie, at least, only called upon this device in dire extremities, when single-stage mechanisms proved insufficient, I consider it to be the usual form of S-R learning. And furthermore, taking Hull's suggestion about symbolism very seriously, I have tried to show that the representational character of the mediation process provides the basis for a theory of sign behavior — or, if you will, of cognition.

We may start with the fact that certain stimulus events have a "wired-in" association with certain response events; for the hungry infant the taste and feel of warm milk in the mouth are reflexly associated with swallowing, salivating, and digestive activities, and the pressure of a yielding object against the lips is reflexly associated with sucking and head-turning. This type of stimulation I call a *significate*. However, since I want this class to include previously learned as well as wired-in relations, I would define a significate as *any stimulus that, in a given situation, reliably elicits a predictable pattern of behavior*. Thus all unconditional stimuli in Pavlov's sense are significates, but the reverse is not true. Now, there is an infinitude of stimuli that are *not* initially capable of eliciting specific patterns of behavior — the sight of the breast or the infant's bottle does not initially produce salivating, for example. Under what conditions will such a pattern of stimulation become a *sign?*

I would state the conditions this way: *whenever a nonsignificate stimulus is associated with a significate, and this event is accompanied by a reinforcing state of affairs, the nonsignificate will acquire an increment of association with some fractional portion of the total behavior elicited by the signifi-cate.* I call such fractional behavior a representational media-tion process. It is representational because although now elic-ited by another stimulus it is part of the behavior produced by the significate itself — this is why the bottle becomes a sign of milk–food object and not any of a thousand other things. It is mediational because the self-stimulation it produces can become associated with various overt responses appropriate to the object signified — sight of the bottle can thus mediately evoke "yum-yum" noises and reaching out the arms. Just what portions of the total behavior to the significate will appear redintegratively in the mediation process? At least the follow-ing determinants should be operating: (1) *energy expenditure* — the less the effortfulness of any component of the total be-havior elicited by the significate, the more likely is this com-ponent to appear in the portion elicited by the sign; (2) *in-terference* — the less any component interferes with on-going instrumental (goal-directed) behavior, the more likely it is to be included; (3) *discrimination* — the more discriminable any component from those elicited by other signs, the more likely it is to be included. There is considerable evidence in the conditioning literature that certain components of UR, particularly "light-weight" and autonomic components, ap-pear earlier in the CR than other components.

Figure 3 diagrams the theoretical development of *perceptual and linguistic decoding.* We may take as illustration the object, BALL. The large S at the top of the diagram refers to those stimulus characteristics of this object (its resilience, its shape, its weight, and so on) which reliably produce certain total be-havior (rotary eye-movements, grasping, bouncing, squeezing, and even the pleasurable autonomic reactions associated with play-behavior), all of which are symbolized by RT. Now, ac-cording to the mediation hypothesis, the sight of this ball as a visual sensory integration, *initially meaningless,* will come to elicit some distinctive portion of the total behavior to the object as a representational mediation process $(r_m — s_m')$. To the extent that this process occurs, the visual pattern becomes a *perceptual sign* (S) signifying BALL object, e.g., this is *a unit in perceptual decoding.* In other words, here at the ground floor in the development of meaning is the development of perceptual significance. Long before the child begins to use language, most of the sensory signals from its familiar environment have been lifted from their original Jamesian chaos,

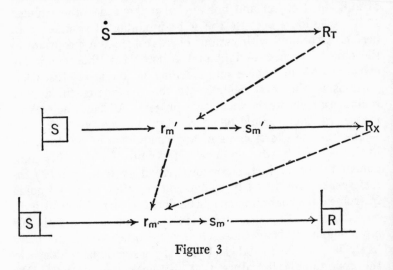

Figure 3

have become perceptual signs of objects by virtue of association with representational portions of the same behavior the objects themselves produce. Incidentally, this seems to carry back one step further the philosophical argument about the nature of meaning; the visual images of objects, rather than being "the things themselves," as is usually assumed, are actually signs whose significance must be acquired.

Now, whereas perceptual signs bear a necessary physical relation to the objects they represent, linguistic signs bear an arbitrary relation. It is characteristic of human societies that adults, when interacting with children, often vocalize those lexical items in their language code which refer to the objects being used and the activities underway. Thus Johnny is likely to hear the noise "ball," a linguistic sign ($\bar{S}$), in frequent and close continuity with the visual sign of this object. As shown on the lower portion of this figure, the linguistic sign must acquire, as its own mediation process $(r_m - s_m)$, some part of the total behavior to the perceptual sign and/or object — presumably the mediation process already established in perceptual learning includes the most readily short-circuited components of the total behavior and hence should tend to be transferred to the linguistic sign. Thus, a socially arbitrary noise becomes associated with a representational process and acquires meaning, e.g., *a unit in linguistic decoding*.

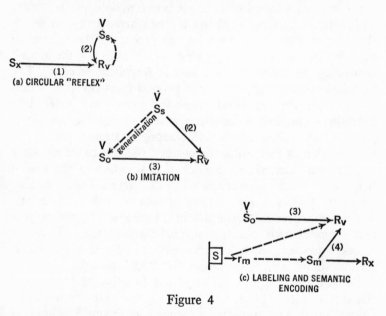

(a) CIRCULAR "REFLEX"

(b) IMITATION

(c) LABELING AND SEMANTIC ENCODING

Figure 4

Figure 4 diagrams the theoretical development of *instrumental and linguistic encoding*. Stage *a*, called "circular reflex," is a necessary first step, because syllable units must become integrated into skills by the practice babbling provides, and the child must be able to repeat its own vocalizations on an auditory feedback basis before it can imitate others. The second step, "imitation," involves nothing more than primary generalization — the tendency to repeat a heard sound spreads from self-produced cues to other-produced cues — and upon hearing mother say "ball" the child says "bah," his nearest skill unit. Now, as shown in stage c, let us assume that the visual stimuli from BALL object already have significance for the child, that is, constitute a perceptual sign by virtue of eliciting a mediation process ($r_m — s_m$) derived from BALL-manipulating behavior. Then the pairing of the heard label "ball" with the perception of the object should have at least the following consequences: (1) a single-stage association between the sight of the object and imitative labeling and (2) a two-stage, mediated association between sight of the object and imitative labeling, as shown by the starred arrow. Whereas the first of these is a meaningless process — sheer labeling that requires the physical presence of the object — the second represents the formation of *a unit of linguistic encoding*. The association of a representational process frees the child's language from the immediate here-and-now — *any* antecedent condition — desire for the object when it is missing, for example — which elicits the critical representational process is now capable of mediating the correct, socially communicative vocalization. This is the essence of abstraction in the use of language, I think. Also indicated in this figure is the fact that mediation processes can become associated with nonlinguistic instrumental reactions (the RX in the diagram); under appropriate conditions of differential reinforcement, the child learns to crawl toward, reach for, and smile at objects perceived as having "play" significance, like this BALL object.

Perhaps the single most important function of representational processes in behavior is as the common term in mediated generalization and transfer. As shown in Figure 5, whenever various stimuli accompany the same significate, they must become associated with a common mediation process, and hence acquire a common significance. Thus, for the rat, the cluster of stimuli surrounding a food object (its appearance and odor, the auditory "click" that announces its coming, the corner around which it is found, and so on) become roughly equivalent signs of the food object. To the extent that these signs have varied in their frequency of pairing with this common significate, they will constitute a *convergent hierarchy of signs* yielding the same significance but with varying strength or probability. Similarly, when a number of different overt responses are reinforced in association with a particular sign or class of signs, they will constitute a *divergent hierarchy of instrumental acts* associated with the same mediator. With any

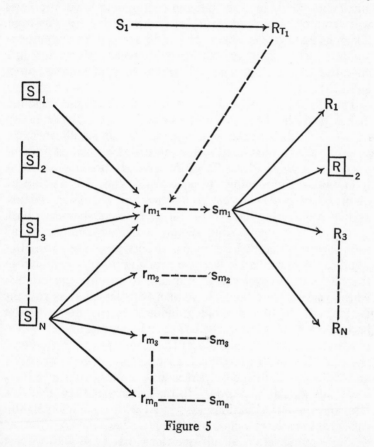

Figure 5

sign having a danger-significance for the rat will be associated a hierarchy of alternatives — running, freezing, turning a ratchet-wheel, and so on. These instrumental alternatives will also vary in their habit strengths or probabilities, and selection among them will depend particularly upon contextual cues. Finally, I have indicated toward the bottom of this figure that signs may come to be associated with *divergent hierarchies of mediators*. If the same set of sensory signals accompanies food significates often, sex significates occasionally, and pain significates seldom, this set of signals will become a somewhat ambiguous sign, in that different representational processes will tend to occur with varying probabilities. In language, homophones like *case, bear,* and *right* are merely extreme examples; here again, as whenever divergent hierarchies are operating, selection depends on context (e.g., conditional probabilities).

The availability of such hierarchies to the mature organism makes possible the tremendous flexibility we observe in behavior. If to a particular sign having a certain significance, the subject learns a new instrumental adjustment, such as pressing a lever or saying "Please," this immediately becomes available to any other sign having the same significance. Here we speak of *mediated generalization*. If a novel set of sensory signals, such as a flickering light in the rat's box or some unusual dark spots on the human's skin, acquire a danger significance, all the previously learned instrumental acts associated with this significance immediately become available to this new sign — the rat will shift quickly to running, to turning the ratchet-wheel, and the like, and the human will immediately call the doctor, talk to his wise old grandmother, rub his arm with bacon grease, or whatever he has already learned to do in situations having this significance. Here we speak of *mediated transfer*. The processes we call cognitive — concept formation and utilization, attitudes, personality traits, problem-solving — fit this mediational model, in the sense that they involve a class of stimulus situations associated with a common significance that mediates a class of alternative behaviors.

There are several difficult questions that arise with respect to the mediation hypothesis. One is this: *is such a two-stage process necessary?* Even at the rat level, there is a great deal of experimental evidence requiring a two-stage interpretation: the separation of learning from performance in many of the investigations inspired by Tolman (33); the role of secondary reinforcement mechanisms in experiments by Mowrer (21),

Neal Miller (20), and others; the evidence for "learning to pay attention" in discrimination studies like those of Lawrence (15). At the human level: in the many studies of semantic generalization, the measured generalization between stimuli like JOY and GLEE obviously depends upon some common (and unobservable) mediating reaction to them, not to any physical similarities in the stimuli themselves (JOY and BOY are much more similar physically); the separation between learning and performance is even more clear in human behavior — witness the changes in attitude that may be produced by quietly watching a television program — and, as far as I can see, the phenomena of meaning and intention, so obviously displayed in human language behavior, entirely escape a single-stage conception. Another question arises: *what is the real nature of representational processes?* Here I have little to say. Following Hull, I have attributed stimulus-producing response characteristics to the process, because in this way it is possible to transfer all the conceptual machinery of single-stage S-R psychology — generalization, inhibition, habit strength, habit competition, and the like — to both the decoding and encoding sides of my two-stage model. However, this does not require a peripheral view as against a central one; the representational process could be entirely cortical, although I suspect it involves peripheral events in its development, at least. And I have no idea as to what might be the neurological basis or locus of such a process. In other words, for the present I am quite content to use the mediation process as a convenient intervening variable in theory, having responselike properties in decoding and stimuluslike properties in encoding.

Another critical problem is that of *indexing these representational processes,* particularly in humans. If we index the occurrence and nature of representational processes by the very behavior presumably mediated by them, we run full tilt into the circularity which I believe characterized Tolman's theory. What we need is some index of representational states that is *experimentally* independent of the behavior to be predicted. In other words, we need some way of measuring *meaning.* Most of my own experimental work at Illinois over the past five years has been devoted to this problem, and what follows is a very concise summary.

To measure anything that goes on within the little black box, it is necessary to use as an index some observable output from it. From a previous survey (22) of varied outputs that are to greater or lesser degree indicative of meaning states — ranging from minute changes in glandular secretion and motor tension to total acts of approach, avoidance, and the like — we conclude that language output itself provides the most discriminative and valid index of meaning. After all, this is supposed to be the function of language. But what linguistic output gains in sensitivity and validity it seems to lose on other grounds; casual introspections are hardly comparable and do not lend themselves to quantification. What we need is a carefully devised *sample* of linguistic responses, a sample representative of the major ways in which meanings can vary.

The *semantic differential,* as our measuring technique has come to be called, is a combination of association and scaling procedures. We provide the subject with a standardized sample of bipolar associations to be made to each concept whose meaning is being measured, and his only task is to indicate the direction of his association and its intensity on a seven-step scale, for example, the concept LADY might be checked at step "6" on a *rough-smooth* scale, signifying "quite smooth." The crux of the method, of course, lies in selecting the sample of descriptive polar terms. Fortunately — and contrary to the assumptions of some philosophers — the myriad dimensions available in language are not unique and independent; our basic assumption is that *a limited number of specific scales, representative of underlying factors, can be used to define a semantic space within which the meaning of any concept can be specified.*

This points to *factor analysis* as the logical mathematical tool. Two factor analyses have already been reported (25); although they were based on the same set of 50 descriptive scales (selected in terms of frequency of usage) one involved Thurstone's Centroid Method and the judgment of 20 concepts against these scales by 100 subjects and the other, by

40 subjects, involved forced pairing among the verbal opposites themselves, with no concepts specified, and a new factoring method developed by my colleague, George Suci. Both analyses yielded the same first three factors: *an evaluative factor,* identified by scales like *good-bad, clean-dirty,* and *valuable-worthless;* a *potency factor,* characterized by scales like *strong-weak, large-small,* and *heavy-light;* and an activity factor characterized by scales like *active-passive* and *fast-slow.* A third factor analysis, based on a sample of 300 scales drawn from Roget's *Thesaurus,* 20 varied concepts, and the judgments thereof by 100 subjects, has just been completed (with the aid of ILLIAC, the Illinois digital computer, without which this work would have been impossible), and again exactly the same first three factors appear in order of magnitude. The regularity with which the same factors keep appearing in diverse judgmental contexts encourages us to believe that we are getting at something fairly basic in human thinking.

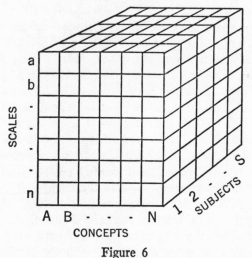

Figure 6

Although this factor work is interesting in its own right, its purpose is to devise efficient measuring instruments for meaning. In practice, small sets of scales, heavily and purely loaded on each of the factors isolated so far, are combined as an instrument against which subjects rate signs of any type — ordinary verbal concepts, the self-concept and other-concepts, cartoons, art objects, TAT or Rorschach cards, attitude objects, and so on. As shown in Figure 6, application of such an instrument to a group of subjects yields a cube of data, each cell of which contains a number from 1 to 7 (the seven-step scales), each column of which contains a profile for a given concept, and each slice of which represents the complete profiles for all concepts for a given subject. The *meaning of a concept* to a given individual or group is operationally defined as the profile of numbers, or means, in a single column or, more efficiently, as the point in the factor space determined by this profile. *Difference in meaning* (between two concepts for a given subject or group, between two individuals or groups for a given concept, or between two testings) is operationally defined by D (distance) $= \sqrt{\mathrm{E}d^2}$, the generalized distance formula. Figure 7 illustrates allocation and distances among three concepts — HERO, SUCCESS, and SLEEP — within the three-factor space so far derived. All three concepts are favorable evaluatively, but whereas HERO and SUCCESS are simultaneously quite *potent* and *active*, SLEEP is quite *impotent* and *passive*. The use of multivariate D has the additional advantage that all distances between concepts judged against the same set of scales can be represented simultaneously in the space defined by the scale factors. Computing the D-values between each concept and every other concept yields a distance matrix which, when only three factors are involved, can be plotted as a solid model. Such models represent, if you will, bits of "semantic geography," and the changes in such structures over time and across individuals or groups yield interesting descriptive data. Doctors Suci and Tannenbaum and I are now working on a monograph that will summarize the methodological and descriptive research with the semantic differential to date.

Is this instrument a valid index of representational processes in human subjects? Information on this point is much harder to come by. There is no doubt that this instrument, as far as it goes, measures meaning in the colloquial sense: the meanings of common adjectives are differentiated in obvious ways, expected differences between Republicans and Demo-

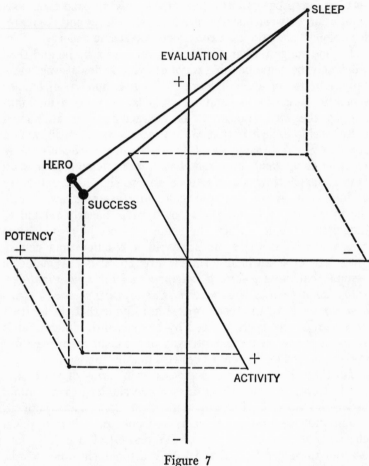

Figure 7

crats are revealed, and so on. We also have some evidence that the dimensions we have isolated by factor analysis correspond to those used spontaneously by subjects in making meaningful judgments — an experiment by Rowan (28) showed that the similarity relations within a set of concepts obtained with the semantic differential corresponded closely with those obtained for the same subjects by the method of triads (where dimensions of judgment are not specified), and other studies of this sort are in progress. But this offers only the most tenuous connection between our measurement procedures and the repre-sensational mediator as a construct in learning theory.

Let me suggest what I think this relation may be and then what may be some possible ways of tying it down experimentally. Our factor analytic work indicates a number of bipolar semantic dimensions — and such bipolar opposition in thinking, by the way, appears to be characteristic of all human cultures. My hunch is that *the representational mediator is a complex reaction made up of a number of components, these reaction components corresponding to the semantic factors we have isolated.* Now, we have been able to show that extremity of judgment on our semantic scales (for example, away from the midpoint, "4," toward "1" or "7") is linearly related to judgmental latency, when the same subjects judge the same concepts against the same scales in a reaction-time device. Since latency is an index of habit strength, it is reasonable to assume that *more polarized judgments on the semantic differential correspond to stronger habits associating sign with mediator components.* In other words, I am saying that the location of a sign in the space defined by the semantic differential is an index of the nature and intensity of the component reactions making up the mediation process elicited by that sign.

Do these identifications make sense in terms of what data we do have? For one thing, the profile similarities we obtain between signs are obviously dependent upon some implicit, meaningful reaction to the signs and not upon their physical characteristics — profiles for LADY and GIRL are very similar, but those for LADY and LAZY are not (in other words, the instrument is indexing a two-stage, semantic process). Secondly, note the responselike nature of the three factors we have isolated so far — *evaluation* (general autonomic reaction?), *potency*, and *activity*. If representational mediators were in truth fractional portions of total behavior, one would expect them to have responselike characteristics. In this connection, I may mention another factor analysis we have done, on the communicative meanings of 40 posed facial expressions. Again three factors accounted for most of the common variance, and these were identified as *pleasantness* (for example, from GLEE down to ACUTE SORROW), *control* (from CONTEMPT over to HORROR), and *expressiveness* (from COMPLACENCY out to the whole array of active expressions like CONTEMPT, RAGE, and HORROR). These *look like* the same factors, and they are clearly related to the reactive natures of emotional states.

We have planned a number of experiments to check this bridge between semantic measurement and representational process. One is a straightforward *mediated generalization* study — if my hunch is valid, then the measured similarity between signs, as obtained with the semantic differential, should predict the amount of mediated generalization between them under the usual conditions. Another variant of the same design will compare two types of *bilinguals:* compound bilinguals (who have learned two languages in such a way that translation-equivalent signs are associated with a single set of meanings) against coordinate bilinguals (who have learned two languages in such a way that translation-equivalent signs are associated with a double set of somewhat different meanings). Again, profile similarities between translation-equivalent signs obtained with the semantic differential should predict mediated generalization, compound bilinguals showing greater generalization than coordinate bilinguals.

Figure 8 provides a summary picture of the model I have been describing. Projection, integration (both evocative and predictive), and representation levels on both decoding and encoding sides of the behavioral equation are indicated, as well as the S-R relations within each level. The labels given to each type of association or "pathway," such as "pure semantic decoding" and "grammatical encoding," reflect my major interest in language behavior, but, as I have implied throughout this paper, to the extent that this picture is valid it should hold for perceptuo-motor sequences as well. This is admittedly

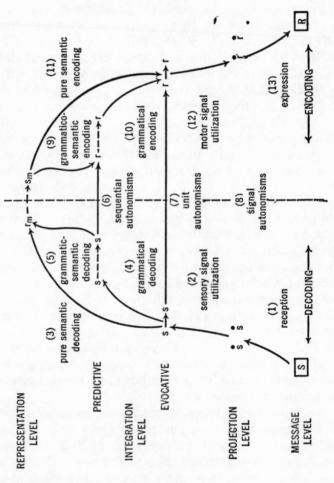

Figure 8

a complicated conception of behavior, but I doubt that any conception sufficient to handle the complexities of language is going to be very simple. Although I have not indicated it in the diagram, for reasons of clarity, it should be assumed that there are hierarchies of alternatives of varying probability at each locus of S-S, R-R, and S-R relations.

We have made one check on the over-all validity of this model. This was an attempt to predict the greater-than or less-than contingencies between various language disturbances in *aphasia*. Suppose that we were able to get inside the full-blown mechanism shown here and cut one or more of the pathways — perhaps right across pathways 5 and 9, connecting grammatical predictive integrations with representational processes — what should happen? On the decoding side, all language performances requiring one to get the significance of sequences of signs should be lost (for example, understanding complex commands, reading interpretively, and the like); on the encoding side, the grammatical correctness of intentional speech should be lost, producing *telegraphia*. On the other hand, both the significance and the ability to produce isolated semantic units should be preserved (pathways 3 and 11), as should previously learned automatisms, like reading aloud mechanically and reciting a familiar poem. Working with the detailed reports of some 35 classic aphasia cases, two clinical graduate students (who were completely unfamiliar with the theory) and I noted in each case the presence and absence of disturbance in some 20 different language performances (such as reading aloud, labeling, written word recognition, speech skills, and so on). Empirical contingencies between performances over these cases were then computed and compared with contingencies predicted from theoretical analysis of the "pathways" essential to each performance — the greater the overlap in "pathway" utilization, the more likely it is that disturbance of one would be accompanied by disturbance in the other. A nonparametric test of correspondence between predicted and obtained contingencies was significant beyond the .001 level. While such results do not confirm the details of our theoretical model, they do seem to substantiate the general analysis into several levels of organization and two stages of decoding and encoding, and they have also encouraged us to work on some new aphasia tests based on the model.

Perception and Meaning

I would identify as "perceptual" those phenomena characteristic of both evocative and predictive *integrations in decoding,* including direct effects upon this level from the projection system and indirect, "feedback" effects upon this level from the representational system. Actually, this way of thinking about perception agrees pretty well with the ideas of other psychologists: Bruner (3) draws a distinction between "autochthonous" and "behavioral" determinants, the former referring to retinally dependent events and the latter to cognitively dependent events like values and meanings, as I understand it; Hebb (8) distinguishes between "sensory" and "non-sensory" figures on what appears to be the same ground; and Gibson (5) distinguishes the "anatomical visual field" from the "ordinal visual world," again on the same grounds, as I read him. And although I deliberately have not as yet read Floyd Allport's new book on perception, I expect that the same distinction will be found there.

Why *is* there this agreement about dual control over perceptual process? It is perfectly clear from empirical data that what the subject reports as his experience depend both upon the stimulus information given to his senses and upon the store of information derived from past experience. Stimulus information, as operated upon by mechanisms in the projection system itself, determines what sensory signals are present at any moment. These sensory signals set limits upon the possible integrations that can occur. *Stored information* is of two sorts: (1) the entire past history of sensory signal pairing has resulted in hierarchies of evocative and predictive integrations within this level itself, integrations that tend to fill out sketchy sensory information (closure) and predict synchronous and successive events in proportion to their environmental probabilities; (2) because certain cognitive states have accompanied some but not all integrations within competing hierarchies, the self-stimulation arising from such cognitive states will facilitate or increase the probability of these perceptual integrations as against others. I imagine that these "feedback" effects from the representational system operate just like other sensory signals, and exert their selective effect upon alternative integrations simply by virtue of their past contingencies with exteroceptive signals. Effects of motivational states upon perception could be handled in similar fashion.

A beautiful demonstration of this is to listen to an unfamiliar chorus from Gilbert and Sullivan, alternately either following the printed libretto or merely listening without the printed guide. While the reader is seeing the printed words, the *auditory* information seems perfectly intelligible, yet the moment he looks away from the text it degenerates into gibberish. I believe it is feedback from decoding of the printed words that operates selectively among alternative auditory integrations. Now let me apply this type of analysis to two specific perceptual problems, recognition and constancy.

Identity and Recognition in Perceiving. Identifying or recognizing something requires that sensory signals activate a representational process; this must be so, it seems to me, because it is this process that mediates encoding of the words by which the subject reports his perceptions. Before he can express any "hypothesis" as to *what* the input information represents, some cognitive process must occur. I think Ames, Cantril, Kilpatrick, and the others associated with the "transactional" point of view have the same thing in mind when they say (12, p. 4), ". . . we can only have a sense of objective 'thatness' when the impingements on our organism give rise to differentiated stimulus-patterns to which differentiated significances can be related." What is missing from their treatment of perception, however, is any analysis of the nature and development of such signifying processes. Earlier in this paper I described one conception of how stimulus patterns acquire significance or meaning.

Accepting the notion that recognition of "thatness" depends upon the arousal of a representational process in the perceiver, we may now ask what classes of variables should, in theory, influence the probability of recognition. The first class of variables is so obvious that most students of perception have taken it for granted, although the human engineering people have been very much concerned — this is *the availability of the sensory signals themselves* (projection level). The probability of "detection" (usually a kind of recognition) varies with the intensity of sensory signals generated by the physical stimulus, which can be modified by manipulating exposure time, changing the receptor population, moving the stimulus, and so on. The laws operating here are those characteristic of the projection system. What subsequent integrations can occur is limited by this sensory information — a circular pattern of high intensity has about zero probability of being decoded as a vertical line.

For just this reason, in studying the effects of higher-level determinants upon recognition we usually reduce the clarity of the sensory input. A second class of variables concerns *the availability of alternative sensory integrations* (integration level). As has been demonstrated repeatedly (compare Howes, 9; Howes and Solomon, 10; and others), with intensity-duration factors held constant, the probability of printed-word recognition is a very regular function of frequency of usage, which is another way of saying frequency of sensory signal pairing in past decoding experience. George Miller and others at M.I.T. (17) have demonstrated the same sort of thing for intelligibility (recognition) of spoken words, and I believe one could interpret Gestalt data on "goodness of form" in the perception of figures along similar lines. The laws operating here would be those characteristic of the integrational system.

We can also specify *availability of representational processes themselves* as a class of variables. One relevant experiment is reported by Brown and Lenneberg (2). These investigators first measured the availability of labels in the English language code for various patches of color (a patch of one wave length would be consistently and quickly labeled, yet one of a different wave length would be inconsistently and slowly labeled); they then demonstrated that in a recall situation ease of recognition of color patches by different subjects was predictable from the previously measured availability of their labels. Many other experiments (which I shall not cite in detail) illustrate how *representational feedback* selects among alternative perceptual organizations, how significance helps determine recognition. When frequency-of-usage factors are held constant — a necessary control — it can still be shown that recognition times for words and visual forms vary with such things as values, attitudes, previous rewards or punishments, and the like.

I would like to say something, however, about "perceptual defense." The obvious problem is this — how can an organism defend itself against perceiving a threatening stimulus when the threat depends upon first decoding the significance of the stimulus? Earlier in this paper I suggested that mediation processes are composed of a number of reaction *components*, corresponding to the factors of meaning, and that the associations of these components with a sign will vary in habit strength. Now, since probability of reaction is a function of habit strength, it follows that those meaning components having the strongest habit strength will tend to be elicited at shorter exposure time than those having weaker habit strength. In general, since *fully* discriminated meaning (recognition) depends upon the total semantic profile, this implies that as exposure time is increased the meaning of any sign should develop gradually: the blur produced by H-A-P-P-Y should first yield a vaguely favorable impression, then a more specific favorable-active impression, and should finally be recognized. With signs that have a dominantly threatening significance, *this* component should be aroused first, prior to complete decoding. If the subject is set for complete decoding, the resultant flood of anxiety self-stimulation could well muddy up the sensory waters and delay further decoding operations (perceptual defense). On the other hand, should the subject be alerted for danger signals, the same prerecognition anxiety stimulation could serve as a distinctive cue in selecting among alternatives (vigilance). And for *any* sign, the dominant component should, through its feedback signals, facilitate alternative integrations of "hypotheses" having similar significance (value resonance). These notions are testable in a number of ways.

The Perceptual Constancies. I have already discussed how a perceptual sign, such as the visual image of an object, may acquire its significance. Now, by virtue of the fact that physical objects and the organisms that explore them are changeable and moveable, the sensory signals deriving from objects will be variable through certain dimensions. The infant's bottle will appear in various sizes as distance changes, in various shapes as the angle of regard changes, in various brightnesses and hues as the intensity and composition of illumination changes. However, the variable sensory integrations arising from the same physical object under different conditions eventuate in the same terminal behavior and hence acquire a *common significance* — retinal images of various sizes, shapes, qualities, and intensities which derive from the infant's bottle as an object are repeatedly followed by milk-in-mouth, and hence acquire a common representational process. According to this view, then, *constancy in perception is the association of a common representational process* (significance) *with a class of stimulus patterns variable through a number of physical dimensions.* In the language of the "Transactional School," this is a common "thatness" shared by a class of stimulus patterns.

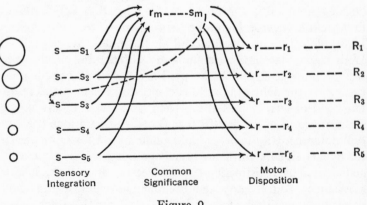

Figure 9

This is by no means the whole story. In the course of inter-action with environmental objects, the members of such stimulus classes become associated with different instrumental sequences and hence with *differential motor dispositions*. Figure 9 may clarify what I have in mind. The sensory integration arising from an APPLE very close to the face $(s - s_1)$ is identified as this edible object (common significance), but comes to be associated with mouth-opening and biting sequences, and hence the motor integration or disposition toward such behavior $(r - r_1)$. The integration characteristic of APPLE held at crooked arm's length $(s - s_3)$ has the same perceptual meaning, but is associated with dispositions toward grasping or flexing the arm. And the tiny retinal image characteristic of APPLE across the room $(s - s_5)$ — again signifying this same edible object — has become most strongly associated with locomotor approach movements. In other words, the sensory integrations deriving from familiar objects become associated with both common representational processes and differential motor dispositions; the former constitute identity or "thatness" in perception and the latter constitute "thereness" in perception, part of the unconscious syntax of adjustive behavior.

It should be noted that, as shown in this diagram, selection among alternative "therenesses" or behavioral dispositions depends upon signals from both the integrational and representational systems. The disposition toward grasping requires both that the visual angle be of a certain size *and* that it be identified as a particular known object — given the same visual angle, an apple will be grasped at and a beach ball run after. On the other hand, sensory integrations arising from meaningless, abstract, or unfamiliar objects, or objects of variable size like balloons, will be associated ambiguously with various motor dispositions. The many observations by the Princeton group, summarized by Kilpatrick (12), on absolute distance judgments are consistent with this view. Familiar and standard-sized objects like playing cards and cigarette packs were accurately judged as to distance when only size cues were available, but unfamiliar or abstract stimulus objects like star points and oak leaves were not. Similarly, when size and distance cues are put in conflict, apparent size will tend to be constant while apparent distance varies *if* the object is identified as a familiar thing having a "real" size.

But what, psychologically, *is* the "real" size of an object? Thouless (32), for example, says that constancy always consists in a "regression toward the real object," but he says little indeed about what this "real object" is or how it is established. Let me suggest an experiment and its result. We will project lifelike images of various objects onto an invisible screen at an unknown distance from the observer so that they seem to hang out there in empty space. By some optical means, we will allow the observer to adjust the physical size of these images until they seem "natural" or "just right" in apparent size. Knowing the actual distance of the screen and the final objective size of the image, we will compute the visual angle subtended by each object-image when judged to be "natural-looking." We will find that these visual angles correspond very closely to those subtended by these same objects at their ordinary inspection distances. We inspect and compare horses and automobiles at a distance of some 20 feet; we compare cigarette packages at crooked arm's length; we inspect the sharpness of record needles at a distance of about 6 inches. In other words, *the "real" or "natural" size of an object will be found to be the visual angle subtended at which the finest visual discriminations for that class of objects can be made*. I would also be willing to bet that this "natural" visual angle will approximate a constant for all objects, dependent upon retinal characteristics. The same argument would apply to all other dimensions along which constancy operates — the "real" color and brightness of an object will be that experienced under white light of normal daylight intensity; the "real" shape of an object will be that experienced when held perpendicular to the line of regard (because this is the condition for finest shape discriminations); and so on.

Now, from all this it follows that the representational mediation process associated with a particular class of signs, which gives them their "appleness," "horseness," "pack-of-cigarettesness," or what-have-you, will be most frequently and strongly elicited by that sensory integration corresponding to the "real" object. This is to say that we will most often be decoding the perceptual significance of an object when it is being inspected in that portion of the visual field where the finest discriminations can be made, when we are "paying attention to it." By the same token, as shown by the dashed arrow in Figure 9, *the feedback self-stimulation from this representational process must be most strongly associated with "tuning-up" or predicting this "real" or normative sensory integration.* From this we can derive a number of the standard phenomena of constancy. (1) What is perceived is usually a compromise between the "real" behavioral object and the actual sensory information. Recognition of a meaningful object will itself, through feedback, change the sensory signals in such a way as to increase the probability of occurrence of a more "normal" perceptual integration. Obviously, the less intense and clearly defined the retinal signals, or the more intense the feedback signals from the cognitive system, the greater should be this tendency toward normalizing. Therefore, (2) the phenomenal characteristics of familiar, meaningful objects should show greater constancy than those of nonsensical, unfamiliar, or abstract objects. "Object-colors" show constancy, but "film-colors" do not; a dinner plate held at various angles shows more constancy than forms cut from white cardboard. And similarly, (3) the more natural the situation in which constancy is measured, or the more motivated the subject toward behaving with respect to "things," the greater is the constancy shown. Adults, children, monkeys, and even fish display almost perfect constancy in going about their everyday affairs. In other words, the ordinary behavior of organisms is concerned with decoding the *significance* of signs, regardless of their momentary physical characteristics, and with encoding intentional behavior that takes account of these significances.

Summary

I said this paper would be speculative, and I think I have kept my word. In order to discuss the topic I originally proposed, I found it necessary to present a rather general theory of behavior, and despite the length of this paper my treatment has been a very sketchy one. The theory conceives of behavior as a two-stage process, decoding the significance of received signals and encoding intentions into overt acts. Both decoding and encoding processes are assumed to involve three interactive levels of organization — a projection level, an integration level, and a representation or cognitive level — but the principles governing one level do not seem to apply to the others. Throughout this paper I have tried to demonstrate the essential identities of perceptuo-motor behavior and language behavior when viewed within this framework, and I at least feel that both become more understandable by virtue of being compared.

I am not unaware of the crudeness of this kind of theorizing. It is certainly more programmatic than rigorous and more qualitative than quantitative, but, on the other hand, I think that for some time to come rigorous, quantitative theories in psychology are going to be feasible only in very restricted areas. And in the meantime, many of us are going to want to do what we can with such complex problems as perception and language. Theories such as the one I have outlined can help to systematize what information we do have, can provide an impetus to new research, and can give us at least the illusion of some understanding.

BIBLIOGRAPHY

1. Attneave, F. Some informational aspects of visual perception. *Psychol. Rev.*, 61:183–193 (1954).
2. Brown, R., and E. Lenneberg. A study in language and cognition. *J. abnorm. soc. Psychol.*, 49:454–462 (1954).
3. Bruner, J., and C. C. Goodman. Value and need as organizing factors in perception. *J. abnorm. soc. Psychol.*, 42:33–44 (1947).
4. Bruner, J. S., and L. Postman. On the perception of incongruity: a paradigm. *J. Personal.*, 18:206–223 (1949).
5. Gibson, J. J. *The Perception of the Visual World.* Boston: Houghton, Mifflin (1951).
6. Fairbanks, G. Selected vocal effects of delayed auditory feedback. *J. speech hear. Disord.*, in press.

7. Hake, H. W., and R. Hyman. Perception of the statistical structure of a random series of binary symbols. *J. exp. Psychol.*, 45:64–74 (1953).

8. Hebb, D. O. *The Organization of Behavior*. New York: Wiley (1949).

9. Howes, D. H. On the interpretation of word frequency as a variable affecting speed of recognition. *J. exp. Psychol.*, 48:106–112 (1954).

10. Howes, D. H., and R. L. Solomon. Visual duration thresholds as a function of word-probability. *J. exp. Psychol.*, 41:401–410 (1951).

11. Hull, C. L. Knowledge and purpose as habit mechanisms. *Psychol. Rev.*, 37:511–525 (1930).

12. Kilpatrick, F. P. (ed.). *Human Behavior from the Transactional Point of View*. Hanover, N. H.: Instit. for Assoc. Research (1952).

13. Köhler, W., and H. Wallach. Figural after-effects. *Proc. Amer. Phil. Soc.*, 88:269–357 (1944).

14. Lashley, K. "The problem of serial order in behavior." In L. A. Jeffress (ed.), *Cerebral Mechanisms in Behavior*. (The Hixon Symposium) New York: Wiley (1951).

15. Lawrence, D. H. Acquired distinctiveness of cues. II. Selective association in a constant stimulus situation. *J. exp. Psychol.*, 40:175–188 (1950).

16. Marshall, W. H., and S. A. Talbot. "Recent evidence for neural mechanisms in vision leading to a general theory of sensory acuity." In H. Klüver (ed.), *Visual Mechanisms*. Lancaster, Pa.: Cattell (1942).

17. Miller, G. A., G. A. Heise, and W. Lichten. The intelligibility of speech as a function of the context of the test materials. *J. exp. Psychol.*, 41:329–335 (1951).

18. Miller, G. A., and J. A. Selfridge. Verbal context and the recall of meaningful material. *Amer. J. Psychol.*, 63:176–185 (1950).

19. Miller, G. A., L. Postman, and J. S. Bruner. Familiarity of letter sequences and tachistoscopic identification. *J. gen. Psychol.*, 50:129–139 (1954).

20. Miller, N. E. Studies of fear as an acquirable drive: I. Fear as motivation and fear-reduction as reinforcement in the learning of new responses. *J. exp. Psychol.*, 38:89–101 (1948).

21. Mowrer, O. H. *Learning Theory and Personality Dynamics*. New York: Ronald (1950).

22. Osgood, C. E. The nature and measurement of meaning. *Psychol. Bull.*, 49:197–237 (1952).

23. Osgood, C. E. *Method and Theory in Experimental Psychology*. New York: Oxford Univ. Press (1953).

24. Osgood, C. E., and A. W. Heyer. A new interpretation of figural after-effects. *Psychol. Rev.*, 59:98–118 (1951).
25. Osgood, C. E., and G. J. Suci. Factor analysis of meaning. *J. exp. Psychol.*, 50:325–338. Urbana: Univ. Illinois Press (1955).
26. Postman, L., J. S. Bruner, and R. D. Walk. The perception of error. *Brit. J. Psychol.*, 42:1–10 (1951).
27. Riesen, A. H. The development of visual perception in man and chimpanzee. *Science*, 106:107–108 (1947).
28. Rowan, T. C. Some developments in multidimensional scaling applied to semantic relationships. Ph.D. thesis, Univ. of Illinois, 1954.
29. Senden, M. von. *Raum-und Gestaltauffassung bei operierten Blindgeboren vor und nach der Operation.* Leipzig: Barth (1932).
30. Sperry, K. W. "Mechanisms of neural maturation." In S. S. Stevens (ed.), *Handbook of Experimental Psychology.* New York: Wiley (1951).
31. Taylor, W. Application of "cloze" and entropy measures to the study of contextual constraint in samples of continuous prose. Ph.D. thesis, Univ. of Illinois, 1955.
32. Thouless, R. H. Phenomenal regression to the real object. *Brit. J. Psychol.*, 21:339–359 (1931).
33. Tolman, E. C. *Collected Papers in Psychology.* Berkeley: Univ. Calif. Press (1951).

DISCUSSION

David Rapaport

THE scope of Dr. Osgood's paper is such that an adequate evaluation of it would require a careful study of his reference points. Since I did not undertake such a study, I will comment on only a few points.

We know from Dr. Osgood's other writings that he is interested in looking into the gap between the stimulus and the response, that he is inclined to pry open the lid of that "little black box," and that he is dissatisfied with a psychology of the empty organism. Here he restates his stand, offering many statements of facts and ideas rarely seen in papers entitled "A Behavioristic Analysis . . ." Perhaps the most striking one is the statement that S-R theories "say little or nothing" about the integration of either sensory or response events, and that "both sensory and motor signals are capable of becoming organized." True, many behaviorists have said something like this. Lashley and Hebb did, and Tolman's cognitive maps, as well as Hull's habit-family-hierarchies, are organizations of this sort. But Dr. Osgood seems to go further. He speaks of an experience-determined increase in the *stability* of such integrations, of a transfer to *central programing* of the function of these integrates, of evocative integrations functioning as *units,* of "S-R relations originally organized on the 'voluntary' level . . . becom[ing] *autonomous integrations,*" and of a syntax of behavior. I believe that the implications of all these statements become particularly clear when Dr. Osgood (like Piaget) lets some of these integrations develop from a *"circu-*

lar reflex," and when he speaks of hierarchies of signs, of instrumental acts, and of mediators, and asserts that "the *availability* of such hierarchies to the mature organism makes possible the tremendous flexibility we observe in behavior." To me all this sounds very much like what Allport is concerned with when he speaks of functional autonomy, and like what psychoanalytic ego-psychology calls autonomous structures of the ego. It seems to me that Hebb (the similarities to whose theory Dr. Osgood duly indicates) was involved with the same issues when he took such pains to show how it is that his neural circuits, assemblies, and phase sequences do not "extinguish," though they are not "reinforced." If we take these statements and their terms (integration, structure unit, autonomous integration, hierarchy, availability) at their face value, then we must judge that Dr. Osgood's conception departs considerably from the "habit" conception of behavior phenomena, in which the major — if not the only — guarantee of stability and availability is overlearning.

To my mind, Dr. Osgood's three levels and two stages are one way of taking a forthright stand against the psychology of the empty organism, that is, one way of conceptualizing what goes on in that little black box. They are an attempt to furnish the empty organism. Thus functionalism seems to allow some room for structural considerations, and many an idea that a while ago could have been dismissed as "emergentist" nonsense is lent respectability or conceptual status. I have in mind particularly Dr. Osgood's "units" and "autonomous integrations." I think it would be correct to suggest that S-R theorists refuse to conceptualize many familiar characteristics of cognition which they cannot (or should we say cannot as yet?) reduce to S-R linkages, while Dr. Osgood is ready to conceptualize such characteristics. I think this is a great advance. It seems that even if Dr. Osgood is convinced of the ultimate reducibility of all behavior phenomena to R-R, S-R, and S-S linkages, he still feels that one must take cognizance of the phenomena and of their interrelationships before starting the process of reduction. Indeed, it seems to me that Dr. Osgood implies that whatever the origin of such units, structures, hierarchies, and integrations, and whatever ultimate concepts they might be reducible to, it will not change the fact that they seem to have abiding roles of their own. But I must not go further; I may be substituting my hopes for Dr. Osgood's intentions.

Let me turn, however, to those points of the paper which I do not consider an advance. Dr. Osgood assumes that he can derive his rather complex furnishings of the "black box" from associative linkages established by frequency. This is disappointing; the integrations, units, and so on, that Dr. Osgood attempts to conceptualize deserve to be conceptualized first of all because they show that stability, availability, et cetera, of which Dr. Osgood's paper speaks. As I see it, the crux of the issue is this: can an association — or conditioning — theory support such a stability? How do the "structures" in question escape the fate of time decrement or extinction; or, if they do not escape it, whence their stability and availability? How is a relationship, established by the vanishing glue of conditioning, capable of integrating other "neural events"? Let me put it this way: in every behavior, both the content and the intent must be taken into account. When I grab a paper, I both grab the *paper* and I *grab* the paper, that is, I experience both the paper and my act. While — if we try very hard — we might be able to deal with the contents (here the paper) without an abiding structural point of reference, we cannot do so in dealing with the act (that is, the grabbing, which makes me a grabber). Brentano's acts, Claparède's *moiité*, Head's and Bartlett's schemata, Hebb's phase sequences, in psychoanalytic theory Erikson's "modes," all refer to such stable reference points. The hope of basing this stability of structures on conditioning reminds me of the hope of playing a successful croquet game *à la Alice in Wonderland*, with flamingoes for mallets and hedgehogs for balls. But the associationist croquet game is even more hopeless because it seems to exclude the assumption of a player capable of compensating for the vagaries of his flamingoes and hedgehogs.

It may be appropriate to bring in an epistemological consideration. When we postulate a furnished rather than an empty organism, we shift from a *tabula rasa* conception of the mind to one of a mind that has a nature of its own. Dr. Osgood's structures, units, and hierarchies are steps away from the *tabula rasa* conception. The difference is like that between clay, which can be readily molded, and marble or wood, where you have to go with the grain. In spite of all the furnishings Dr. Osgood has provided it with, his world seems to remain a Hume-ian world, in which behavior is determined by the probability distributions of environmental events, and even the choice of structuralized alternatives is probabilistically regulated. This is particularly striking when Dr. Osgood, in speaking of anticipations in language and illustrating his point by experiments on filling in missing words of sentences, explains the results in probabilistic terms: "At each point in a language message . . . we have a hierarchy of structural alternatives . . . varying in their probabilistic character with the grammatical restrictions in the language as a whole." But there is an alternative explanation of the results of such experiments, according to which the filling of a gap in a sentence is the effect of a series of progressively narrowing anticipations, regulated by "relevance," rather than by probabilistic hierarchy. The results so far do not rule out either of these explanations. What I mean is this: an adaptive organism's behavior is adaptive in that it meshes into environmental probability. Thus probabilistic findings do not necessarily prove that the furnishings of the "little box" are built by the laws of associative frequencies and probability. Max Delbrueck, the biophysicist, has pointed this out. He cautioned the physicist dealing with biological phenomena that adaptive regularities must not be mistaken for laws of nature. The psychological theorists who "follow Hume" seem to me to make this very mistake. They conceive of a mind that has no autonomy. One of the basic problems of psychology as a deterministic science is how to account for the observed relative autonomy of the organism from its environment. I think this is the problem Tolman attempted to solve in his *Purposive Behavior*. Hume-ian conceptions do not account for such observations. While it is difficult to see how associationism of any vintage can account for this relative autonomy, it is incumbent on us not to discount the possibility that it might do so, until it is proven that it cannot. What disquiets me is that Dr. Osgood does not face this issue.

However, let me abandon this epistemological aside and turn to Dr. Osgood's three levels and two stages. I know very little about the nervous system, and thus should tread gingerly here; yet this 2 x 3 seems to be too neat. Studies by Heinz Werner and Piaget in the last twenty years give the impression that the two stages so neatly separated by Dr. Osgood are actually indivisibly intertwined — particularly in the early phases of human ontogeny. Werner's sensory-tonic theory, as well as Piaget's derivation of all "intelligence" from sensory-motor intelligence, raises the question of whether or not this sharp separation of "encoding" and "decoding" is simply the intellectual heir to the S-R frame of mind, even if it is much more thoughtful and rich than its parent.

But how about the three levels? Again my limited knowledge of perceptual-neurophysiological facts and theories makes me hesitant. Yet am I altogether mistaken when isomorphism as the first law of the "projection level" reminds me of Hume, Locke, and so on, according to whom clear and simple ideas are valid representations of the objects perceived? Dr. Osgood speaks about Jamesian chaos and about visual images not being things but only signs whose significance must be acquired. Surely this is an advance over the pragmatic, naïve realism of older behaviorism. But is it an entirely mistaken impression that the neat separation among the three levels militates against the study of the very process by which the visual image emerges from the Jamesian chaos and acquires significance? At any rate, the development of the constant object — as described by Piaget in his "Construction of Reality" — suggests an intertwining of these three levels. Would not also the phenomena of physiognomic perception and the perception-need relationship raise doubts about such a neat and simple progression in "decoding" and "encoding"?

Dr. Osgood's paper is so rich that it might seem ungrateful to point to any lack in it. Yet it seems important to indicate that he has failed to clarify the role of motivations in his theory of behavior. He tells us that the rules of operation differ from level to level. Should we nevertheless assume that motivations operate by the same rules — that is, reinforcement — on all levels, except for the projection levels, where they would presumably have no role? This lack of clarification of the role of motivations is the more striking since Piaget, as well as Hebb, whose goals are in many respects similar to Dr. Osgood's, also gives only a cavalier treatment to motivations. Two questions arise here. Does interest in the relatively permanent tools of cognition and behavior (the furnishings of the black box) diminish the investigator's interest in motivation? Are the conceptual tools appropriate for dealing with structures prohibitive or at least inhibitive of dealing with motivations, and vice versa? May I point out that a similar antithetic relationship seems to have obtained for a long time between the study of motivations and the study of structures in psychoanalysis. But the fact that I raise this matter may rest on a misunderstanding: Dr. Osgood may be taking the S-R motivation theory so much for granted that he feels no need to waste time on any of this. If so, then I should express my feeling that the place of motivations in a structural theory does need clarification.

Let me end by pointing again to advances. In discussing the selection from "the hierarchy of alternatives," Dr. Osgood — even though his major concern pivots around the most "probable" integration — turns finally to "attentional functions," as did Hebb. He asserts with Hull that it is of the essence of representational processes to produce stimuli. To my mind, these conceptions of attention and representation, if carried to their logical conclusion, are steps towards awarding consciousness a conceptual status. We can see the dim outlines of a concept of consciousness as an organization that has integrative and regulative as well as self-regulative functions, such as attention, representation, and stimulus production.

Just a final word: however critical some of us may be of Dr. Osgood's theory, few will fail to appreciate the advance it represents. Moreover, the clarity of its reasoning, the wealth of information it integrates, and, last but not least, the pertinence and ingenuity of the experiments reported in it command our respect.

THE RELATION BETWEEN
BEHAVIOR AND COGNITION

Leon Festinger
Stanford University

A RECENT article by Scheerer (3) begins, "Cognitive theory might be expected to deal with the problem of how man gains information and understanding of the world about him, and how he acts in and upon his environment on the basis of such cognitions."

This is, to me, a very acceptable statement of what the study of cognition is supposed to do. But the phrase in the above quote, "might be expected to" is used advisedly by Scheerer. The study of cognition has not even begun to fulfill these objectives. Indeed, it has been so lacking that some psychologists, intelligent and able ones, have at times contended that there is no need to study cognition at all. There are many more who have not argued about it, but have simply proceeded to do empirical work without reference to cognition.

To establish the importance of cognition in the science of psychology, simple declarative sentences that assert its value are not sufficient. It is necessary to produce a body of specific theory and data that establish the relations existing between cognition and behavior. General theoretical frameworks will not suffice, either. A system must be put forward of hypotheses directly relevant to data from which specific derivations may be made.

In this paper I shall present one basic hypothesis concerning a relationship between behavior and cognition, explore some of its implications, and present the results of a few studies that test these implications. The material I will discuss is part of a larger theory that I am preparing for publication as a book.

It has frequently been stated or implied that the actions of people are steered or governed, at least in part, by cognition. There is little need to belabor this point. Certainly, if a person is motivated toward some end, the specific actions in which he engages will, in part, be determined by his cognition about his environment and about the paths that will lead to the end he desires. But this states only one aspect of the relation between action and cognition. Equally important is the fact that cognition will be governed and determined, at least in part, by the actions which a person takes. We do not intend here to refer to the rather trivial fact that a person's actions, by bringing him into certain kinds of contact with the environment, will expose the person to new information and new experiences that will be cognized. What we mean is that, if a circumstance should arise such that some cognitive elements do not fit or are not in line with a person's actions, there will arise pressures directed toward changing these dissonant cognitive parts.

To clarify what I mean, let us imagine a person who is a reasonably heavy cigarette smoker. After having smoked for many years he is abruptly informed, in newspapers and magazines, that such heavy smoking markedly increases the likelihood that he will have lung cancer. Let us further imagine or assume that if this person, knowing this, had it all to do over again he would not start to smoke. But what will he do now that he does smoke and knows the deleterious effects of smoking? One answer is simple: namely, he might stop smoking. But there are many, our exemplary person among them, who find that they cannot stop smoking. A highly uncomfortable situation has then been produced: his action persists, he continues to smoke, but there exists an important set of cognitions that do not fit with this action. We may then expect to see evidences of the pressures that will exist to change this dissonant cognition. He will probably attempt to persuade himself that the danger to his health has been vastly exaggerated in the newspapers or that the whole thing has not been proven, that cigarette smoking is really not harmful at all.

These processes do occur. For example, a survey conducted by the Minnesota Poll about six months after the supposed link between cigarette smoking and lung cancer began to receive publicity asked respondents whether or not, and how much, they smoked and also asked them whether or not they believed the link between smoking and cancer had been proven. Let us look briefly at the data separated into four groups: nonsmokers, light smokers, moderate smokers, and heavy smokers. Included in the smoking category are only those who have been smoking for at least a year, that is, began smoking *before* they heard about the link with lung cancer. For these four groups, going from nonsmokers to heavy smokers, the percentage of those who think the link has *not* been proven are, respectively, 55%, 68%, 75% and 86%. In other words, the more they smoke, the greater is their tendency to reject this dissonant cognition.

In the hope that this example has clarified our intentions, we will proceed to elaborate the hypothesis we wish to advance.

The hypothesis states, essentially, that there exists a tendency to make consonant one's cognition and one's behavior.

In order to explain this hypothesis we must spend some time in giving definitions of the terms we will use. There are three possible relations that can exist between items of behavior and items of cognition: consonance, dissonance, and irrelevance. (These same three relations also exist among items of cognition or among items of behavior, but within this paper we shall oversimplify for the sake of brevity.) A relationship of irrelevance exists if a particular item of cognition has absolutely nothing to do with a particular item of behavior. Thus, for example, an irrelevant relation exists between the opinion that elementary schools are overcrowded and the behavior of playing golf on a nice sunny Saturday morning. Such irrelevant relations produce no pressure on persons, and we may, for the rest of the paper, ignore them.

A relationship of consonance exists between a particular item of cognition and some item of behavior if, holding the motivation constant, we find that this behavior should follow on this cognition in the absence of other cognitions and in the absence of restraints. Thus, for example, the knowledge that construction crews are working on a certain street would be consonant with the behavior of taking an alternate route in driving to work. The opinion that it is going to rain would be consonant with the behavior of carrying a raincoat. The belief that thieves are around would be consonant with a feeling of fear when walking home on a dark night.

A relationship of dissonance exists between an item of cognition and an item of behavior if, under the same conditions described in the paragraph above, a different behavior should follow upon this cognition. Thus, for example, the belief that it is going to rain is dissonant with the behavior of going on a picnic. The opinion that some other person is an excellent and careful driver would be dissonant with the presence of a fear reaction while driving with him in the ordinary course of events.

One may, of course, raise the question as to why dissonances ever arise. There are many circumstances in which dissonances are almost unavoidable, and it will help our discussion later to list now some of the ways in which dissonance can occur.

1. *A change in the situation.* A given behavior may have been initially consonant with cognition. A new set of circumstances, however, may arise, which, impinging upon the person either directly or indirectly, produce new cognition that is, at least momentarily, dissonant with the existing behavior.

2. *Initial direct contact with a situation.* A person's cognition may have been formed from communication with others. The first direct experience may impinge on the cognition in such a way as to produce dissonance with the existing behavior.

3. *Simultaneous existence of various cognitive elements.* It is probably a usual state of affairs that there are several relevant cognitive items, some of which are consonant with a given behavior and others of which are dissonant with that same behavior. Under such circumstances it may not be possible for

the person to find a behavior that eliminates all dissonances.

Our hypothesis states that if a relation of dissonance exists there will arise forces to eliminate the dissonance and produce consonance. These pressures to reduce dissonance can act to change the behavior or to change some of the cognitive elements. For our present focus of interest we shall concern ourselves with those situations where the resistance to change of behavior is strong enough so that the existing behavior persists. Under these circumstances the pressure will be exerted mainly on the cognition. For example, should dissonance exist for a person who has recently spent considerable money to buy a new car, considering the resistance to taking a loss on selling it again, the pressures to reduce dissonance would act mainly on his opinions and attitudes toward this and other cars.

Probably the major ways in which cognition may be changed so as to make it consonant with behavior are by selective exposure to relevant features of the environment which the person hopes will support consonant cognition, and by active attempts to influence others to provide support for these cognitions. Thus, for example, a person who is afraid of riding in airplanes may avidly read and remember every account of an airplane disaster which he comes across and may avoid hearing about or reading about safety records and the like. Or let us imagine a person who has bought a new car just prior to the introduction of some new improvement. He may very actively try to persuade his friends that this new improvement is useless, will not work, and adds unnecessarily to the expense of a car. If he succeeds in persuading them he will then have support for a cognition consonant with his possession of a car that does not have this new improvement.

To summarize the statements involved in the preceding discussion we may say that: (1) the existence of dissonance between cognitive elements and the individual's actions produces pressures to reduce or eliminate this dissonance; (2) when the action itself is difficult to change, or when change in action would not serve to reduce the dissonance, these pressures are manifested mainly in attempts to alter the cognitive elements.

Thus far, of course, these hypotheses have little specificity.

There are many questions that must be answered before we can relate these hypotheses satisfactorily to the empirical world. How do we identify the existence of dissonance? How do we measure degrees of dissonance? How can we measure the manifestations of the pressure to reduce dissonance?

The best way to answer some of these questions briefly, and to make the connections between these hypotheses and the observable data one might collect, is to spell out the operational definitions and the implications in connection with specific studies that test the theory. This we will proceed to do.

Dissonance Resulting from Decisions

Let us briefly consider the circumstances of making a decision and then analyze the situation after the decision has been made. While we shall discuss the matter with reference to a decision between two attractive alternatives or courses of action, the analysis may be easily generalized to any decision situation.

Presumably, if a person is faced with a choice between two alternatives both of which have many desirable features, he goes through a process of examining each alternative, weighing each against the other, and then choosing that course of action that seems more desirable to him. But what can we say about the state of affairs after the decision has been made? The individual has made a choice and has committed himself to one of the two possible courses of action. All the information and knowledge he has concerning the desirable aspects of the chosen course of action is, of course, consonant with his present behavior. But in the process of making the decision he also acquired considerable information concerning attractive and desirable features of the course of action that he later rejected. These cognitive elements are now dissonant with the action he did take. Hence, dissonance is an almost inevitable consequence of having made a decision. The magnitude of the dissonance that will result from the decision is dependent upon the importance to the person of the decision and on the attractiveness of the rejected as compared to the chosen alternative.

If such dissonance does exist, our hypothesis would lead us

to expect some evidence of pressures to reduce the dissonance. Let us then examine how, in a postdecision situation, these pressures might manifest themselves.

There are many possible manifestations into which we do not have time to go here. We shall, however, explore one such manifestation that is particularly relevant to the data we shall describe. Clearly, one way in which the postdecision dissonance may be reduced is by emphasizing the importance and the desirability of the chosen alternative. Consequently, to the extent that the attempts to reduce dissonance are successful, we would expect to observe, after the decision, an increase in the discrepancy between the attractiveness of the two alternatives involved in the choice. Raising the attractiveness of the chosen alternative and/or lowering the attractiveness of the rejected alternative would be evidence of successful attempts to reduce dissonance. The degree to which such postdecision changes occurred would presumably depend upon the magnitude of dissonance that existed initially.

Brehm (1) designed and conducted an experiment to test these implications of the dissonance hypothesis under controlled conditions. His procedure was as follows: eight objects, each of which had a retail value of about twenty dollars, were assembled. They included objects like an automatic toaster, a small radio, an art book, and the like. Each subject, on coming to the laboratory, was told by the experimenter that the latter was doing some advertising research for a number of manufacturers. The experimenter was very apologetic to the subject for asking her to spend her time on this type of research since it would have very little educational or interest value for her. However, the manufacturers had agreed, the experimenter said, to provide some things that could be given to the subjects to recompense them for their time.

The subject was then asked to look over the eight objects that had been assembled and to rate each one on an eight-point scale in terms of how attractive and desirable it was. The scale ranged from 1, highly undesirable, to 8, extremely desirable. After the completion of this initial rating the experimenter told the subject that she would be given one of these objects as the gift from the manufacturer. Since the experimenter wanted to be sure that they didn't run out of any single product and also wanted to be sure, he said, that each subject got something she liked, he had prepared a system whereby each person was given a choice between two objects. He then designated two of the objects and asked the subject to pick the one she wanted as her gift. The one chosen was wrapped up and put with the subject's belongings.

The two objects were selected by the experimenter with reference to the subject's ratings of their desirability. One of the two objects had been rated either 5, 6, or 7 by the subject: that is, toward the desirable end of the scale. The other object was, in the condition designed to produce high dissonance, always rated just one scale step below the object that the subject would presumably choose. In the condition designed to produce low dissonance the other object was two or three scale steps below the chosen one. Thus, by experimental manipulation, once the person had made the choice, two degrees of dissonance had been created.

The experimenter then proceeded to show the subject brief evaluations of four of the eight objects. Each of these evaluations contained a mixture of good and bad points about the particular object it described. For half of the subjects in each condition, two of these evaluations concerned the objects between which they had chosen. For the remainder of the subjects, none of the evaluations concerned those objects that had been involved in their decision. Thus, within both the high and low dissonance conditions, half the subjects received no additional information about the objects involved in the choice and hence no help in reducing dissonance. The other half did receive new information that, potentially, they could use to reduce dissonance.

Following their reading of these evaluations and telling the experimenter what they considered the salient features of each, they were asked to rate each object again on the same scale on which the original rating was made, but on a different sheet.

The true purpose of the experiment was then explained in detail to the subjects. Unfortunately the subject could not actually be given the valuable gift since the financial resources of graduate students are limited. The subjects all appreciated the explanation and understood the purpose of the experiment before they left.

The relevant data for us to look at are the changes in the rating of desirability of the objects from the initial rating to the final rating, which was made after the subject had chosen one of the two objects to keep. A rise in the attractiveness of the chosen alternative and a decline in the attractiveness of the rejected alternative were scored as positive changes. Figure 1 presents, for each of the four conditions, the average amount of change in the attractiveness of the two objects involved.

It is clear in Figure 1 that, as we expected from the hypothesis of pressures to reduce dissonance, the increase in discrepancy between the alternatives is greater for the high-dissonance conditions than it is for the low-dissonance conditions. In the "no-information" conditions — that is, where the subjects were given no evaluations of the objects that were involved in the choice — the increase in discrepancy is + .86 for the high-dissonance condition and only +.45 for the low-dissonance condition. In other words, in the high-dissonance condition the two alternatives, initially rated 1 scale unit apart, are 1.86 scale units apart on the second rating. In the low-dissonance condition the alternatives, initially 2½ units apart on the average, are almost 3 units apart on the second rating.

Since it is possible that these changes might be simply the result of repetition and statistical regression, it is necessary to compare these changes with the changes of rating of objects which were not involved in the decision. The solid bars in Figure 1 show the change in discrepancy that occurred for those objects not involved in the decision which had similar initial ratings to those that were involved in the decision. These changes were calculated separately, on the basis of the regression equations, for those objects not involved in the decision and about which the subjects read no evaluations and for those not involved in the decision about which the subject did read evaluations.

It is clear that, for the no-information condition, the change for those objects not involved in the decision is slight and actually in the opposite direction. For the high-dissonance condi-

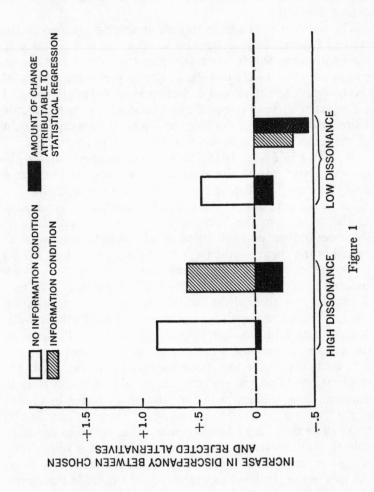

Figure 1

tion the expected change for objects not involved in the decision is —.06 and the comparable figure for the low-dissonance condition is —.15.

Let us now look at the results for the conditions where the subjects did read evaluations of the objects that were involved in the decision. Here it must be remembered that the evaluations that they read were rather mixed, half good and half bad, and hence the effect was to lower the second ratings of objects that had initially been considered attractive and to raise the second ratings of objects initially considered unattractive. In other words, the over-all effect was to bring the evaluations of the objects closer together. This can be seen from the solid bars on the figure. For those objects *not* involved in the decision and initially rated similarly to the alternatives in the high-dissonance condition, the expected change would be —.18. The comparable figure for the low-dissonance condition is —.48. The change for the alternatives that were involved in the decision is —.36 for the low-dissonance condition, a figure indistinguishable from the expected regression. The information, tending to be derogatory, has completely eliminated the effect for this group. In the high-dissonance condition, however, the change is +.60. Again, in spite of the effect of the evaluations the subjects had read, the discrepancy is increased for the high-dissonance condition, although not quite as much in the no-information condition.

It is clear, then, that there is a difference between the high- and low-dissonance conditions in the increase in discrepancy between the alternatives after the decision is made. One would also expect that with some information present, the subjects would be able to make use of this information to reduce dissonance when such pressures were present. We might then expect that the difference between the high- and low-dissonance conditions would be greater in the information condition than in the no-information condition. This is, indeed, the case although the difference fails to be statistically significant.

We may conclude, however, that the implications from the dissonance hypothesis seem to be supported. The closer the alternatives are to one another, the greater the postdecision dissonance and the greater the pressure to reduce this dissonance by increasing the discrepancy between the alternatives.

Dissonance Resulting from Public Compliance

Let us now consider another type of situation that frequently produces dissonance between cognition and behavior. It sometimes occurs that for one reason or another a person publicly exhibits behavior or makes verbal statements with which, privately, he does not agree. We shall examine one type of situation in which this occurs, briefly look at the implications of our hypotheses, and then examine the data from an experiment relevant to these implications.

Let us imagine that a person is asked to state publicly his opinion concerning some issue. Under most circumstances, where no particular pressure is applied on this person to say one thing or another, he will publicly state an opinion corresponding with what he privately believes. He might, however, be offered, explicitly or implicity, some reward for publicly stating an opinion at variance with his private opinion. Presumably, if the expected reward is large enough — that is, larger than the resistance to making a public statement with which he does not agree — he will make the required public statement in order to obtain the reward.

If the person does exhibit such public behavior at variance with his private opinions, then those cognitive elements corresponding to his private opinion are dissonant with the action he has taken. On the other hand, of course, the knowledge of the reward he will obtain represents cognition that is quite consonant with his action. We can then say something about the magnitude of the dissonance that will result from such public compliance and, hence, about the magnitude of the pressures that will exist to reduce this dissonance.

If we consider the amount of dissonance as relative to the amount of consequence that exists, then clearly the maximum possible dissonance between the public behavior and the dissonant private opinion would exist when the public behavior is elicited by the smallest reward necessary to produce it. Since the knowledge of the reward to be obtained is consonant with the action taken, as the magnitude of the reward increases, if we hold constant the importance of the issue and the resistance to showing the public behavior, the magnitude of dissonance decreases.

Following our hypothesis, we would then expect to be able to observe some manifestation of pressure to reduce dissonance following public behavior that is at variance with private opinion. One obvious way in which such dissonance may be reduced is to change one's private opinion so that it coincides more closely with the publicly stated opinion. One consequence we might look for, then, is that public compliance without private acceptance, such as might be produced by the offer of a reward for the compliant behavior, would be followed by a change in private opinion. Since the pressure to reduce dissonance is itself a function of the magnitude of the existing dissonance, we would also expect that, as the reward used to elicit the public compliance increases, the amount of change in private opinion following the public statement would decrease. If the reward were very large there would be very little dissonance and we would expect very little opinion change, if any.

An experiment by Kelman (2) provides a very adequate test of these implications of the hypotheses concerning a cognitive dissonance. In this experiment, seventh-grade children were asked to write essays favoring one of two types of comic-book stories. Some days before and, again, some days after these essays were written, measurements were obtained concerning their private opinions of these two types of comic books. Three conditions were used in the experiment, each condition offering a different magnitude of reward to the subjects if they wrote essays favoring one of the two types of comic-book stories. The conditions follow.

Condition 1. This condition probably is the one offering the smallest reward for public compliance. As will be seen, it is a little difficult to decide whether this condition or Condition 2 offers a smaller reward. My own hunch would be that Condition 1 offers a smaller one. In this condition the subjects were told that if they wrote essays favoring comic book A, they would get a free copy of the book *Huckleberry Finn*. If, however, they wrote essays in favor of comic book B they had a chance to win a free pass to the movie "Huckleberry Finn." There were only five free passes for that class and so each child could not be sure of winning the pass, but he had a chance. The experimenter had previously determined that seeing the movie was more attractive than receiving a free copy of the book. It is also likely that the chance of obtaining the movie pass was more attractive than the certainty of receiving a free book, but probably only slightly so. The net effect of this condition then is to urge the subjects to write in favor of comic book B, the reward being a chance at a free pass to a movie minus the certainty of receiving a free book.

Condition 2. In this condition the children were told that they would receive a free copy of the book *Huckleberry Finn* if they wrote essays favoring comic book A. Nothing was offered if they wrote favoring comic book B. The effect, then, of the instructions was to urge them to write essays favoring comic book A, the reward being the certainty of getting a free book. In my opinion, the certainty of getting a free book is probably somewhat more attractive than is an uncertain chance of seeing a free movie when this would involve losing the free book.

Condition 3. In this condition they were again offered a free copy of *Huckleberry Finn* if they wrote favoring comic book A but, if they wrote favoring comic book B they would also get the book and in addition would definitely get the free pass to the movie. The net effect of this condition, then, is to urge them to write essays favoring comic book B, the reward being the certainty of getting a free pass to the movie if they complied. Clearly, this is the strongest reward of the three conditions.

We have then three conditions, each of which offers a different magnitude of reward if the subjects will exhibit a specific public behavior. In each condition we would expect there to be some who would comply in order to obtain the reward.

As a result of this compliance, there would be dissonance for these people between what they privately think and what they have done. This dissonance would be greatest where the reward offered was comparatively small and would be least where the reward offered was greatest. Thus the dissonance would be greatest in Condition 1 and least in Condition 3. We would likewise expect the pressure to reduce dissonance to be greatest in Condition 1 and least in Condition 3. Since the pressure to reduce dissonance would result to some extent in a change of private opinion we would expect greatest change of private opinion in Condition 1 and least change in Condition 3. The solid line in Figure 2 shows the data on change of

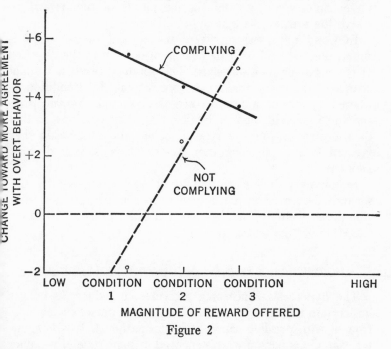

Figure 2

private opinion from before to after the experimental session for those subjects in each condition who complied, that is, wrote essays favoring the story type for which they would obtain the best reward. Clearly, as we expected, the greater the reward offered for compliance, the smaller is the change of opinion in the direction of the compliance shown.

But let us also consider the data represented by the broken line in Figure 2. These data are for those subjects who did not comply, that is, who wrote essays undoubtedly agreeing with their private opinions, thereby giving up the reward that was offered. For these subjects, too, there is dissonance, but it is the obverse of the dissonance that exists for those who did comply. For the noncompliant subjects, their private opinions are consonant with the overt behavior they have shown, but the knowledge of the reward they have given up is dissonant with what they have done. It consequently follows that, for these subjects, the greater the magnitude of the reward refused, the greater the dissonance.

In Condition 1, then, where the reward they refused is slight, there should be little change of opinion in the direction of the behavior they did show. The obtained result is a slight change actually in the opposite direction. In Condition 3, where they give up a large reward, there should be strong pressures to reduce dissonance by changing their opinions, so that their preference for the type of comic book they said they favored is even stronger than before. This is, indeed, what happens.

In summary, it is clear that for those who comply, the dissonance decreases as the offered reward increases. For those who do not comply, the dissonance increases directly with the magnitude of the offered reward.

Information-seeking in the Presence of Dissonance

The hypothesis concerning pressures to reduce dissonance has certain implications for the behavior of persons when confronted with possible sources of information. Let us imagine, for example, a person who is engaged in some type of behavior to which he is, in one sense or another, committed. That is, it is difficult to change the behavior. The person's reaction to possible sources of information relevant to this behavior would then depend in the following ways upon the degree of dissonance that existed between his behavior and cognition.

1. If the cognition is largely consonant with the behavior in question there will be little motivation (considering this source alone) to acquire new information. In these circumstances, then, we should observe little or no voluntary exposure to sources of relevant information. On the other hand, there should be no active avoidance of information, either.

2. If there exists appreciable dissonance between cognitive elements and the behavior in question, there should be active effort to reduce the dissonance and to avoid increasing the dissonance. Thus, if a source of information is seen as potentially reducing the existing dissonance, the person will expose himself voluntarily to this source. If, on the other hand, the source of information is seen as likely to increase the dissonance between his cognition and his behavior, we would expect him actively to avoid exposure to this source of information.

3. If the dissonance achieves a magnitude that makes it greater than the resistance to behavior change, the person would be expected to change his actions. In this manner the dissonance becomes effectively eliminated since, after the behavior changes, those cognitive elements that were dissonant with the old behavior are consonant with the new behavior. If the dissonance that exists is almost, but not quite, large enough to overcome the resistance to changing the behavior, we might observe a relatively peculiar circumstance. In such a situation the easiest way to eliminate the dissonance might be to increase it temporarily. If the dissonance were increased to a point where the behavior changed, the dissonance would be eliminated. In such situations — that is, where the existing dissonance is very large but not quite sufficient to overcome the difficulty of changing behavior — we might expect persons to expose themselves to dissonance-increasing sources of information.

In order to test these theoretical implications of the dissonance hypothesis, an experiment was designed to fulfill three specifications.

1. The subject must be put into a situation where he will engage in continuous behavior that has some appreciable resistance to change. Change of behavior must, however, be clearly possible.

2. The experience of the subject while engaging in this behavior is to be experimentally manipulated. Through this experience different subjects should acquire cognition of varying degrees of dissonance with their behavior.

3. At a certain constant point in the course of the experimental session, each subject must be given a free opportunity to examine information relevant to the behavior.

The experiment was conducted as follows. When each subject came to the laboratory, he was told that we were interested in studying gambling behavior and had consequently devised a two-person card game in which the subject would play against the experimenter. Each subject was given two-and-a-half dollars as payment for being a subject, but he was informed that this was the money with which he would gamble. The game, which was simple, was then described to him. A deck of cards would be shuffled and seven cards turned up. The face values of these seven cards would be totaled and, depending upon the sum, either player A or player B would win. The subject was told that he would play thirty trials of this game. Before each trial, no matter which side of the game he was on, he would state how much he wanted to bet on that trial. He was permitted to bet anywhere from five cents to twenty-five cents on each trial.

He was then instructed that the two sides were not equally good, one side having a better chance to win than the other. Since we wanted to be fair, we would allow him to think the situation through, do any calculating he wanted to, and then pick whichever side he wanted to play on. Further, if at any time during the course of the thirty trials he decided he wanted to switch to the other side, he could, but switching would cost him a dollar. This, of course, was all the more reason for him to think carefully and make the correct choice at the beginning. After the subject made his decision, the play started and proceeded for twelve trials.

At the conclusion of the twelfth trial, the experimenter temporarily halted play and showed the subject a graph that purported to show the exact probability for obtaining, by chance, each of the possible totals of seven cards. The experimenter explained to the subject how, using the graph, he could easily calculate the exact probabilities of winning or losing for Player A and Player B in the game which, it will be remembered, was still to be played for another eighteen trials. After explaining the graph thoroughly, the experimenter gave it to the subject and said:

"This graph belongs to you from now on. You may use it or not use it; it is entirely up to you. You may spend as much time with it as you choose. Whenever you are ready to start playing again, just let me know."

The experimenter then waited until the subject indicated that he wanted to resume play. The exact time spent by the subject in looking at the graph was recorded. At this point the subject was told that the experiment was actually finished, and its purpose was explained to him. In payment for his participation in the experiment each subject was allowed to keep the two-and-a-half dollars with which he started. Let us now go back and see how the situation fulfills the conditions we listed previously as necessary for testing the implications of our hypothesis.

1. *Creating resistance to change of behavior*. The subject was told that one side of the game was more advantageous, and he made his own considered decision as to which side he wanted to play on. There is consequently some resistance to admitting he was wrong. In addition he knew that it would cost him a dollar to change sides. There is, then, considerable resistance to changing once he has made his choice.

2. *Producing dissonance between cognition and behavior*. The behavior in question here is, of course, continuing to play on the side of the game which the subject initially chose. The subject's cognition relevant to this behavior is determined in large part by the experiences he has during the play of the game. In the normal course of events, by the end of the twelfth trial some subjects would have won and others lost money to

varying degrees. Since we wanted a considerable range, the operation of chance was assisted here by removing some low cards or some high cards from the deck, depending upon whether we wanted to increase the chance of the subject's winning or of his losing. Thus, at the time the graph was introduced, subjects ranged from those who had won on almost every trial to those who had lost on almost every trial. Subjects who had won had, of course, cognition that told them they were indeed playing on the better side, cognition that was consonant with their behavior. On the other hand, subjects who had lost a lot had acquired cognition that was dissonant with continuing to play on the same side. The magnitude of the dissonance would, of course, be dependent on the consistency with which their experience told them that the side they were playing on lost. In other words, there had been experimentally created a range of magnitude of dissonance between what the person knew about the game and his behavior.

3. *Introducing an opportunity to acquire information.* The graph presented to the subject at the end of the twelfth trial is clearly and obviously an opportunity for the subject to obtain complete and accurate information relevant to the behavior in which he is engaging. His expectations of what the graph will tell him will, of course, be in part determined by what he has learned in playing the game. The amount of time spent by the subject in looking at the graph should be an indication of the eagerness with which he desires to acquire such correct information about the situation.

The data we wish to examine are those pertinent to the relationship between the magnitude of dissonance that exists for the subject at the time the graph is made available to him and some measure of the desire on the part of the subject to expose himself or to avoid exposing himself to this source of information. For the latter variable, desire to acquire information about the situation, the best we can do is a measure of how long the subject spends looking at or making calculations from the graph. This is admittedly a crude measure; that is, some subjects can calculate faster and understand the graph better than others. Nevertheless, on the average, it should reflect adequately what we want.

The measure of the magnitude of dissonance between what the person knows and his behavior can be taken directly from the experience the subject has had during the first twelve trials. It is reasonable to assume that these subjects are sufficiently in contact with reality so that their experiences affect their cognition veridically. Since the subject was allowed to vary his wager, the best measure to reflect this impact on his cognition seemed to be the subject's total winnings over the twelve trials divided by the average amount of his wager over those trials. Losses would then appear as negative numbers. The larger the index, the more consonant would his cognition be with his behavior. The smaller the index of winnings the greater would be the dissonance.

The implications of the dissonance hypothesis for the relationship between these two variables is clear. Let us review them briefly.

1. When the cognition is largely consonant with the behavior — that is, for positive values of the winnings index — there should be relatively little time spent on the graph.

2. When cognition is appreciably dissonant with the behavior — that is, for small to moderate negative numbers of the index — the subject would spend considerable time looking at the graph if he thinks the graph will yield information that will reduce dissonance. If he thinks the graph will increase dissonance, he should spend little time looking at it.

3. For very large negative values of the index he may look at the graph in order to increase dissonance sufficiently to change his behavior.

Figure 3 presents the obtained data with the index of dissonance along the abscissa and time spent on the graph along the ordinate. The figure shows the average time spent on the graph split into nine intervals of dissonance index values. It seems clear from the figure that when cognition is consonant, the amount of time spent on the graph is relatively small. It increases to a peak of slightly more than 300 seconds when the

index value is in the interval from −1.0 to −3.0. This, of
course, represents moderate dissonance but with the experience
of losses being sufficiently inconsistent so that the subjects may

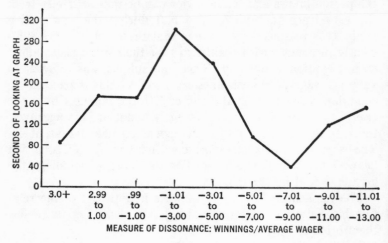

Figure 3

realistically hope that the information obtained from the graph
would reduce dissonance. That is, they may hope that the
graph will tell them that, after all, they are indeed playing on
the correct side.

As the dissonance increases past this point, however, the
time spent on the graph falls off until it reaches an average
of only slightly more than 40 seconds in the interval from
−7.0 to −9.0. Here, of course, there is marked dissonance between what they know and what they are doing. Their experience, however, has been so consistent that they can only expect
the information obtainable from the graph to confirm what
they already know and hence to increase their dissonance.
These subjects have, after all, in twelve trials lost about eight
times their average wager. Expecting that looking at the graph
would increase their dissonance, they scarcely look at it.

It is also apparent that, as dissonance increases further, the
amount of time they spend on the graph increases again. These
last two points on the abscissa certainly represent near-maxi-

mum obtainable dissonance. After all, an index of −12.0 would usually represent losses on every one of the twelve trials. These subjects, then, are probably so close to changing their behavior that they look at the graph in order to help themselves change. Actually, 60 per cent of the subjects in these last two intervals announce, after seeing the graph, that they want to change. This is comparative to 36 per cent of other subjects who have been losing. While this is not conclusive, it is in the direction we would expect. Probably the reason we obtain as high a ratio as 36 per cent of the others wanting to change after seeing the graph is that the graph the subjects were given, if interpreted correctly, would always tell them they were playing on the wrong side. Thus, many of those with moderate dissonance, looking at the graph for a long time in the hope of reducing dissonance, would have perceived the full implications of the graph and would have changed. Indeed, as many as 10 per cent of those who have been winning change after looking at the graph.

It seems clear that the relationship between dissonance and exposure to new information, while complicated when expectations concerning what the source of information will yield are left uncontrolled for the subjects, is consistent with the implications of the hypothesis concerning pressures to reduce existing dissonance.

Summary

Some may feel that the kinds of data we have been presenting do not fit very well into what has traditionally been thought of as the problem area of cognition. For example, in the three studies we have discussed, the dependent variables have been attractiveness of objects, change of opinion, and amount of time spent in looking at a graph. The independent variables have been, respectively, the relative attractiveness of the rejected alternative in a decision situation, the magnitude of reward offered for compliant behavior, and the amount won or lost in a gambling game.

But we are indeed dealing with cognition. We are dealing

with pressures to change cognition and methods of acquiring cognition in a way that makes it possible for us to relate cognition to behavior and to the environmental situation. We have done quite a number of studies relevant to the theory we have described so briefly. The three studies I chose to describe here were chosen purposely to cover a relatively wide variety of situations. If cognition is an important determinant of behavior, a theory about cognition should be found to have relevance to many behavior contexts. Dissonance among cognitive elements or between cognition and behavior can arise in any situation, and, whenever it does arise, certain specific derivations may be made concerning behavior which will be oriented toward reducing this dissonance and concerning the changes that will occur in cognition.

BIBLIOGRAPHY

1. Brehm, J. W. Post-decision Changes in Desirability of Alternatives. Univ. of Minnesota. Ph.D. thesis, 1955.
2. Kelman, H. C. Attitude changes as a function of response restriction. *Hum. Relat.*, 6:185–214 (1953).
3. Scheerer, M. "Cognitive Theory." In Lindzey, G. (ed.), *Handbook of Social Psychology*. Vol. I, pp. 91–142. Cambridge: Addison Wesley (1954).

DISCUSSION

Jerome Bruner

I HAVE a great many comments to make. The first is that subjects in psychological experiments at the University of Minnesota live rather dangerously!

I think Festinger's conception of consonance and dissonance is in a fine and ancient tradition. If you will, it is the psychology of Aesop. The fable of the sour grapes, or one Aesop might have written about a sweet lemon, covers the case very well. I respect the concepts of consonance and dissonance the more for their ancient origin. But if one dips further into folklore and literature, one soon finds that there are interesting cases to the contrary, violations of consonance-dissonance theory like "We look before and after/And long for what is not." That is to say, we sometimes *increase* the pressures on ourselves *after* a decision or choice has been made. Human tendencies are not always so benign as Festinger's formula.

I would like to mention several points where issue might be taken with Festinger. The first of them, which I mention briefly now and to which I shall come back in some detail later, is that Festinger seems to treat action on the one hand and cognition on the other as if somehow they were independent of each other. One of them goes off, the other has to be brought into line, and somehow the cognition that existed before the decision doesn't seem to be related to what happens to the cognition after the decision. Indeed, I would go one step further and say that I think it is characteristic of consonance-dissonance theory that it starts off with an action whose cognitive prerequisites are not stated and then describes cognition only *after* the action. My objection to such a course is that the most interesting aspects of cognition are those that *precede* the making of decisions rather than those that *follow* the making of decisions. Indeed if I had to quote chapter and verse for justifying this assertion I could cite three excellent papers of Festinger's of some years ago on decision processes. Cognition *after* a decision or choice has been made does tend to be reparative and justificatory. Consonance and dissonance do come into play. But is this the general case where cognitive activity is concerned? This leads to my second general objection. (Such an excellent paper can bear having the brickbats thrown before the bouquets!)

I find Festinger's general treatment to be in line with an emphasis that is very much part of our century. According to this emphasis, cognition is a plaything of motivational forces, a justifier of action rather than one of its determinants. The so-called New Look in perception, perhaps, committed the same excess — the notion that cognitions can be indifferently warped and changed to conform to the requirements of action. While this emphasis informs the experiments that have been cited in this book (with the possible exception of the last one), I do not think that it is necessary for the Festinger theory. I would think that insofar as one took into account the problem of what one does cognitively *prior to making a decision,* one is freed from this rather autistic tradition — the idea essentially that cognition is the plaything of action and the plaything of drives. For the easement afforded by consonance-dissonance adjustments is surely related to the adequacy of the cognitive processes that determined the decision in the first place. The chagrin of a poor choice can be eased only slightly by consonance-dissonance processes. I think it is too bad for psychology that in his final paragraph Leon Festinger felt the need to justify or apologize for the inclusion of things like opinions and evaluations in the study of cognition. These are, indeed, at the heart of the study of cognition — what we are all seeking to explain in dealing with such things as coding and decoding or whatnot. I am delighted to see opinions and evaluations brought to the center of the stage, and rather than accepting Festinger's apology, I would like to congratulate him.

His theoretical position, it seems to me, brings into focus the important problem of how an organism deals with conflicts between acting and knowing. His emphasis was upon the way in which one can bring cognition back into line so that one reduces its dissonance with action. One could also deal with strategies whereby action is made consonant with knowledge of a situation. What Festinger is doing is providing a tremendously important link between general psychological processes of cognition and the kind of thing that traditionally concerns the social psychologist and the personality psychologist, too. When we deal with such phenomena as ego defense, we are describing the ways in which a person tries somehow to make his impulse processes consonant with his ego ideal, to eliminate elements which are dissonant and which lead to anxiety. What Festinger has proposed lies astride the junction of general psychology, the psychology of personality, and social psychology.

Let me return to the attack.

First, about the restrospective emphasis in this particular theory — its exclusive emphasis on what happens to cognition *after* one has made a decision. Now let me utter a heresy. I think that on the whole the problem of decision-making, and the utilization of information in decision, has been handled so much more adequately in recent times by theoretical economists than by psychologists that I am a little bit ashamed of our profession. The economists have been forced to deal with such matters — for example, "Shall one invest or shall one not invest on the basis of what is known about the state of the market at a given time?" What I would like to do is to take a little detour into the economist's kind of decision theory (particularly the work of Jacob Marshak), to consider some of the ways in which cognitions *prior* to action might possibly link up with consonance and dissonance processes. Marshak raises the following interesting hypothetical case. Here is an individual who has to make a decision whether to build a bomb-proof shelter or not to build a bomb-proof shelter. The decision about building depends upon his expectation about two possible states of the world — his subjective estimate of the probability of war, on the one hand, and of peace, on the other hand. Now, if you take these two things, the decision alternatives — build a shelter or don't build a shelter — and the two possible states of the world — war and peace — you can construct a pay-off matrix, to use the term of the economists, in this vein. The decisions are "build" and "not build." The possible states of the world are "war" and "peace." Now this gives us a working fourfold table whose cells want filling. If the person decides to *build* a bomb-proof shelter and it should turn out that there is a state of *war* he will be alive and poor. He may have some guilt because of the fact that he did build and other people didn't and might be dead. If he *builds* and there is *peace,* he again is alive and poor but he will surely have regrets. Depending upon your theory of economic values, this regret factor is or is not important. In the event that he does *not build* and there is *peace,* he is alive and rich. Should he *not build* and there is *war,* he is dead.

Now there is your basic pay-off matrix, and Marshak and others propose that values can be given to each one of the possible outcomes. And one can be quite roughshod about these values and assign them ordinal numbers only. Now, what shall the person do under these circumstances? What decision shall he take?

Here arises the question of how one uses information prior to an action, or prior to a decision. The first problem has to do with the values that are given the various outcomes by a decision maker and secondly, of utmost importance, the estimated probability of states of the world — both highly cognitive activities. What if the probability of war in a person's mind is .6 and the probability of peace is .4? Or "war" is .9 and "peace" is .1? Given the assignment of outcome values by the decision maker and given his estimate of the likelihood of war and peace, how does he make a decision? One of the possible "strategies," if you will let me use that term, is a classical one. Its objective is to maximize expected utility. Expected utility is formally computed by multiplying the estimated probabilities of states of the world by the values of the various outcomes, and coming out with the sums for each one of the decisions "to build" or "not to build." Lord knows what expected utility amounts to psychologically! But such an objective will make one be as realistic as possible with respect to the estimates that one is making about the states of the world. One will not trust to the benign after-effects of dissonance and consonance processes, but will get all the best possible newsletters he can get hold of *before the fact* to find out what the states of the world are.

Now there is another kind of strategy that one can employ, one made well known by the work of Von Neumann and Morgenstern. This is the strategy of minimax, so called. Minimaxing refers to minimizing the maximum possible loss that you can possibly undergo as the result of a decision. By minimizing the maximum loss, you essentially take that decision which will help you avoid the thing which has the lowest value, namely death in our hypothetical case. Here one *would* expect cognitive distortions after the fact. It is very likely that there will be a tendency for one who had made a minimax decision to have a gloomy view of the world, for this means essentially distorting his probability estimates of the least favored event upward, making war seem more likely. Now under those circumstances cognition may be made to fit the decision already taken.

We have done some research, for example, on judgmental decision. The so-called "sentry" matrix provides a nice case. In the sentry matrix the individual is put in the position of a sentry having to make a decision whether to shoot an oncoming figure or to withhold fire. The figure approaching can be an enemy or not an enemy; those are the two states of the world. If it is an enemy and the sentry shoots, he saves his own life and he saves the life of his troops. If it is an enemy and he doesn't shoot, under those circumstances he is dead. If it turns out to be one of his own men and he shoots and kills him, he feels regret, but everybody comforts him and says that this man shouldn't have been out there. Now, under conditions of the sentry matrix we find that cognition is distorted in the direction of expecting the most frightening outcome and preparing for it. One cannot trust to the *post hoc* effects of consonance.

Let me come back directly to consonance and dissonance. Festinger's theory is very exciting and obviously fruitful. I think it would be the more so if he linked his *analysis* of what happens after decision to what takes place before decision. Otherwise he will end with a theory of cognition capable of dealing only with hindsight rather than with foresight as well.

COGNITIVE STRUCTURES

David Rapaport

Austen Riggs Center, Inc., Stockbridge, Massachusetts

I

THE relation of cognition to personality is usually treated in terms of motivations. In this paper I shall dwell on another, usually neglected, ingredient of cognition that seems to play a crucial role in the relationship between cognition and personality: namely, *cognitive structure.* By cognitive structures I mean both those quasipermanent means which cognitive processes use and do not have to create *de novo* each time and those quasipermanent organizations of such means that are the framework for the individual's cognitive processes. I shall present three sets of clinical observations and discuss them so as to bring into relief the role of cognitive structures in them. But I shall resist the temptation to present a clinical theory of cognition.[1] I shall try to avoid clinical and psycho-analytic terminology as much as possible, and shall choose the role of the naturalist who describes and sorts out phenomena observed "in vivo," in contrast to the experimenter, whose

---

[1] Cf. Rapaport (87, 88, 89), as well as the "Rationale" sections of Rapaport, Schafer and Gill (93), particularly Part Three, Chapter I. By avoiding clinical theory, I may give the impression in the following that the clinician's only contribution to the theory of cognition is his observations. This is not so. Psychoanalytic theory has not only drawn attention to the phenomena to be described here, but has also offered concepts and theories to explain them. I am deliberately neglecting these theories here. The interested reader will turn to Freud (38, chap. VII; 41, 44, 45), Schilder (100, 101, 102), and Hartmann (57), and will find further references in my own writings referred to above (see also 81).

precise knowledge tested "in vitro" is so often at a great distance from anything "in vivo."

Before turning to clinical observations, it seems necessary to set down some of the general assumptions concerning cognition underlying the discussions to follow. First, a theory of cognition that is broad enough to have clinical relevance must account (a) for man's ways of gaining information about his environment as well as about his needs and other motivations; and (b) for man's ways of organizing the information he has obtained so that it will serve him in controlling and/or fulfilling his needs, and in coping with his environment (see Rapaport, 84, 87). Second, the subject matter of a theory of cognition should include: conscious and unconscious, perceptual and memorial, imaginary and veridical, self-expressive and reality-representing, dreamlike and waking, ordered and freely wandering, productive and reproductive, normal and abnormal cognition (see Rapaport, 88). Third, a theory of cognition must deal both with the processes underlying cognition and with the effects of cognitions on man's behavior. Fourth, a theory of cognition must assume that cognitive processes create some of their components *de novo*, while others are ready-made tools available to them. For instance, a cognitive process may create a new concept but will also use old ones; and the new concept, as well as the method of creating it, may crystallize into tools that will be at the disposal of subsequent cognitive processes. For the moment, it is a moot question whether this transformation, apparently characteristic of our thought processes, of a function into a quasipermanent tool (see Hartmann, 57, and note also the parallel to Allport's conception of "functional autonomy," 4), can or cannot be accounted for by the familiar principles of existing learning theories (see Rapaport, 90, 91). Fifth, a theory of cognition must also assume that both the cognitions and the tools of cognition that emerge from cognitive processes are organized in some quasipermanent and orderly fashion in the mind.

Clearly these last two assumptions pertain directly to the cognitive structures we are concerned with, and here I would like to give a few orienting illustrations.

Memory organizations are perhaps the most common cognitive structures. The classical investigations of memory dwelt primarily on its organizations in terms of spatial and temporal contiguity; early Freudian psychology (39) primarily on its organizations in terms of drives; Bartlett (6) in his conception of schemata, on its organizations in terms of interests and affects. Both the Socratic method of diaschisis and the results of association tests suggest that there is also a conceptual organization[2] of memories: the majority of the popular (most frequent) association-test responses are conceptually related to the stimulus, and these responses constitute about 60 per cent of all the responses of normal subjects in our sample (93, 97).

But memory organizations are not the only cognitive organizations (see Schilder, 101, 102, and Rapaport, 92). Grammar and syntax reflect a great many cognitive organizations. Let us take the modes as our second example. The conditional mode[3] arises rather late in the child's cognitive development. Once it has appeared, its tool or means character is clear, and both our grammar and our sustained capacity to carry on and/or fall back on thought and behavior based on suspended premises show that this tool of thought is an enduring organization.

We shall choose styles as a third example of cognitive organizations. I do not mean merely styles of written prose but cognitive styles in general, including styles of perceiving, conversing, dreaming, and so on. Styles, as cognitive organizations, show striking interindividual differences (see Klein *et al.*, 69,

---

[2] I am using the antithesis of drive organization versus conceptual organization as I used it in *Organization and Pathology of Thought* (88). The choice of the terms is not felicitous. Drive organization is conceptual, too, in the broad sense in which conceptual organization means equivalence organization, and in the narrow sense of physiognomic concept (Werner, 110). Conceptual organization, as I use the term, denotes the equivalence organizations akin to those of logical concepts. The transition between the latter and drive organizations (for example, in terms of physiognomic concepts) appears to be continuous, while my discussion of the antithesis is restricted to the two extreme ends of this continuum.

[3] E. Erikson (29) has described other types of mode organizations of behavior and cognition that originate in body-modes in general or in the modes of "erotogenic zones" in particular.

68, 62). Not that there are no interindividual differences in memory organizations and grammatic-syntactic organizations, too, but these organizations are present in some form, or to some extent, in all members of the species. This is not so with styles. Understatement, for instance, is a familiar style, which in some people becomes a major tool shaping most of their cognitive processes, but may be conspicuously absent[4] in other people. My assistant, Dr. I. H. Paul, is on the track of such style organizations. His experimental subjects tend to use images and ellipsis to the same extent in their recall of a story told to them as in a story that they produce around a given theme. The correlation coefficients (which are around .5 and are highly reliable) suggest that the tendencies to use ellipsis and images are styles that differ interindividually but are stable intraindividually.

I would like to touch on one more problem concerning cognitive tools or means. I have used these terms to designate the ready availability (as against *ad hoc* production) of certain cognitive forms, but I have also implied their usefulness as means to an end. It is obvious that a memory or a concept is a means or tool of cognition; each is one of the means by which we orient ourselves in a problem situation. But it is not so evident how broader cognitive organizations, such as styles, are means or tools of the cognitive process. Let me clarify the point by citing an experiment made by George Klein (67). He used a thirsty and a nonthirsty group of subjects and exposed them to a great number of cognitive (mostly perceptual) tasks and stimuli which involved themes related to thirst. The "New Look" expectation would have been that the thirsty subjects would react differently to these tasks and stimuli from the nonthirsty ones. The results of the experiment did not bear out this simple expectation. However, both the thirsty and the nonthirsty groups were themselves composed of two groups

---

[4] The choice of the examples of cognitive organizations here and in the following may apear to be random and may convey the impression that these organizations form a random assembly. This does not seem to be the case. There is considerable evidence that these organizations are related to each other in that they form multiple complex hierarchies. See Rapaport (86, 88).

of subjects, each representing a perceptual style. Klein called one of these styles "control by constriction," the other "flexible control." In the analysis of the data in terms of this fourfold design (thirsty — flexible control, thirsty — control by constriction, nonthirsty — flexible control, nonthirsty — control by constriction) significant differences emerged. It appears that thirst did influence cognition, but this influence was different in the subjects with flexible controls from influence in those controlling by constriction. Thus, these styles seem to direct or channel the influence of needs or drives, or at least to reflect preferred modes of directing and channeling. This is a familiar situation in clinical practice: the form and direction of drive discharge is coordinated with, if not limited and selected by, defensive organizations. An aggressive impulse defended against by reaction-formation may find expression in excessive altruism; one defended against by projection may find expression in self-protective and provocative maneuvers (see Schafer, 96). This does not mean that style and defense organization are identical, but it does imply that, in the main, both are tools of cognition, used primarily in its dealings with the internal needs of the organism.

A distinction between cognitive processes on the one hand and the structured (patterned and persisting) tools of cognition and their organizations on the other can probably be made by the criterion of rates of change: the processes may be defined as showing a high rate of change, the tools and their organization as showing a low one. In other words, the processes are temporary and unique, the tools and their organizations permanent and typical.

II

Let me begin with a typical example taken from my studies of amnesia (see Rapaport, 86, Gill and Rapaport, 53, Geleerd, Hacker, and Rapaport, 51, Rapaport, 85). An unemployed man leaves his home after a violent quarrel with his wife. Eight hours later he is picked up by a policeman at the Hudson River, a three-quarter-hour's walking distance from his home, his behavior suggesting suicidal intent. Brought to the hospital, he seems quite unaware of his personal identity. This condition lasts ten days and terminates when, in a sodium-amytal interview, he recalls the quarrel with his wife. However, now that he has recovered the awareness of his personal identity, it becomes clear that he has no memory of those eight hours that elapsed between his leaving home and his being picked up by the policeman. Two weeks later, in another amytal interview, he recollects this period also, and describes that during those eight hours he was consumed with rage, guilt, and the idea, "I must end it all." He thought of nothing else and walked the streets scarcely aware of them, barely able to orient himself towards the "end": the Hudson River. A study of the case shows three phases.

(a) *The first eight hours:* the patient's conscious cognition is largely limited to the single idea, "I must end it all," and to the concomitant affects. The patient is apparently incapable of ordered cognition, unaware of his personal identity, but also unaware of this incapacity; Gill and I (86, 53) found in a number of such cases that patients in this phase are, as a rule, not yet aware of this loss of awareness of their personal identity. Fisher's studies (32, 33, 34) corroborate this finding. Janet (64) described such states as monoeideic and polyeideic somnambulisms; others (107, 86) have called them fugues.

(b) *The subsequent ten days:* the patient's ordered everyday behavior and test performance show that he is capable of ordered cognition in general, but that he cannot cognize anything pertaining to his personal identity. Thus he has no awareness of his personal identity. But in the encounter with the policeman he becomes aware — and from then on he remains aware — of this lack of awareness. He shows a certain bewilderment, which increases as he tries to think about his personal identity. This bewilderment is hard to define, though it is distinct from the daze that characterized his behavior at the Hudson River. This phase and its characteristics were first described by Abeles and Schilder (1).

(c) *The final two weeks:* the patient appears capable of all cognitive activities except those pertaining to the first phase, which had been characterized by the loss of awareness of personal identity without an awareness of this loss. This third phase is akin to the familiar retroactive functional amnesias, except for the fact that in this case the period blotted out by the amnesia was itself a special state and this condition, though frequent, is not a necessary part of functional retroactive amnesia (see Rapaport, 86).

Gill and I (86, 53) have found that this sequence and these characteristics of the three phases are typical for such amnesias. Fisher's studies (32, 33, 34) corroborated our findings. We should note that the cognitive processes in each of these phases are sharply distinct from each other as well as from normal cognitive processes. While the clinical study of this case, and kindred cases, shows that the basic drive-motivations underlying the crucial cognitive phenomena of each of the three phases are identical [5] (in this case it is the murderous hostility directed towards the wife), the cognitive contents of the three phases are different. Thus, the first relationship — actually a commonplace one — suggested by this clinical observation is that the basic motivation does not unequivocally determine the cognitive content or, for that matter, the cognitive form.

An inspection of the cognitive contents of these three phases reveals the cohesive character of what can or cannot be cognized in them. By "cohesive" I mean that the contents that are cognized (likewise those excluded from cognition) are not a random assembly, but are selected and held together by discernible unifying principles. The question arises: do the cohesive cognitive contents, which either monopolize cognition or are excluded from cognition in one of the phases of this dis-

[5] I am not implying here that the total motivational constellations of these three phases are identical, nor even that the total motivational constellations of their crucial cognitive phenomena are identical. Under total motivational constellation we subsume also the motivations of defense, control, ego interest, etc., which are obviously at variance in these three phases. All I assert is that the basic drive motivation involved is identical for the "single motif cognition" in the first phase, for the exclusion from cognition of all that pertains to personal identity in the second phase, and for the amnesia in the third phase, for the time span of the first phase.

order, correspond to organizations existing in normal psychological functioning?

Let us consider the first and third phases together. What was cognized in the former and uncognizable in the latter were all cognitive contents related to the motivation represented by the phrase, "I must end it all." This motivation was the aggressive drive that became directed towards the self, and was of such intensity that it excluded all cognitions except some that were relevant to its goal. Thus we are dealing with a cognitive organization centered around a drive.

Do we have any evidence that such cognitive organizations or structures exist in normal psychological life? Bartlett (6) proposed the concept of "schemata" to designate enduring memory organizations as he conceived of them. According to him, these schemata are, to begin with, organized around the special senses, later on probably also around appetites or instinctive tendencies, and still later also around interests, attitudes, and ideals. Bartlett wrote: ". . . because there is . . . notable *overlap* of material dealt with by different 'schemata,' the latter themselves are normally *interconnected*, organized together and display, just as do the appetites, instinctive tendencies, interests and ideals which build them up, an order of predominance among themselves" (p. 212 [italics mine]). Would it be far-fetched to suggest that Bartlett observed, in his studies of normal remembering in "overlapping" and "interconnected" forms, cognitive organizations centered around drives[6] of the very type that pathology shows us here in a skeletonized, isolated form?

I want to refer to further observations supporting this suggestion. When in everyday life an interest, or appetite, or affect becomes overwhelmingly strong, it tends to shed its "overlap"

[6] In terms of clinical theory Bartlett's appetites and instinctive tendencies are probably high-level derivatives of drives. There are cognitive organizations that pertain to and center around these derivatives. Since these derivative motivations are not as peremptory (discharge-oriented) as the basic drives, the cognitive organizations corresponding to them shade more readily into the conceptual organization of memory (see 88). This conceptual organization was for the most part ignored by Bartlett in his study.

and "interconnection" with other interests and appetites. It predominates and even monopolizes, and shows up in the subject's preoccupation with it to the point that he becomes temporarily incapable of cognizing (perceiving and/or thinking about) anything not pertaining to it. Grief and shame, the thought of the beloved or the problem about to be solved, all may grow to this point. We accept these states as normal since, unlike the first phase of our amnesia case, which they resemble, they are not attended by a loss of personal identity and are readily reversible. But we justly characterize people in these states as "obsessed" by their interest or appetite. We encounter the pathological counterpart of these normal preoccupations in obsessional neurotics. In their obsessive preoccupations we find the same limitation of cognition as in the first phase of amnesia and in normal preoccupation, but on the one hand the condition is not readily reversible, and on the other there is no loss of personal identity. However, pathological obsessive preoccupations increasing in intensity lead to obsessional deliria (see Freud, 40), the cognitive character of which is the same as that of the first phase of amnesia: cognition is limited and awareness of personal identity lost, without an awareness of this loss being present. The normal extreme preoccupation with an interest or appetite — to use Bartlett's terms — does produce cognitive conditions and conditions of awareness that appear to be a transition from normal cognition to that of the first phase of amnesia.

We may add that the analyses of slips of the tongue (39), as well as the study of slips of the tongue experimentally produced by means of post-hypnotic suggestion (27, 28), also support the assumption that such drive organizations of cognitions exist in normal psychic life.[7]

Clinically it is easy to show that these drive organizations of memory, by making available as directional indicators both the memories of gratifying objects and gratifications and their

[7] It seems that the experiments of Murphy and his pupils (76), as well as some of the "New Look" experiments in perception (20, 21), have been concerned with some such motivational organization of perception.

contexts, subserve the search for need-satisfiers.[8] Bartlett too seems to imply something of this sort when he maintains that the very factors that build the schemata organize the recall, which he regards as a construction "made largely on the basis of . . . [an] attitude, and its general effect is that of a justification of the attitude" (p. 207).

Let us now consider the second phase of our amnesia case, where cognitions pertaining to the subject's personal identity were not possible though the subject was keenly aware of and bewildered by this loss. The observation implies a loss of cognizability that is not arbitrary but is organized around the subject's personal identity. Is there any evidence that such an organization of cognitions exists in the normally functioning person?

Let us again turn to Bartlett (6). While he takes pains to dissociate himself from any "substantial, unitary self, lurking behind experience" — as I would also — he nevertheless has this to say: ". . . memory, in its full sense, always contains a peculiarly personal reference . . . [because] the 'schemata' and the appetites, instinctive tendencies, attitudes, interests and ideals which build them up display an order of predominance among themselves . . . [and] this order remains relatively persistent for a given organism" (p. 308). But what if this order of predominance is disturbed, as in our case of amnesia? Should we then infer that the "personal reference" becomes interfered with and the cognitions particularly related to it become unavailable? Bartlett has nothing to say about loss of personal identity, but he does refer to a related pathological phenomenon: depersonalization. In depersonalization the cognition of personal identity is not lost but is devoid of

---

[8] See Schilder (100) and Rapaport (92). The drive organizations subserve the search for need-satisfiers primarily by means of signals indicating which need is to be satisfied, in other words by making the need cognizable. They are far less serviceable for cognizing the satisfying object (not to speak of the realistically attainable object). There are two reasons for this. First, these organizations are not based on a hierarchic stratification of cognitions but rather on their equivalence as drive representations. Second, the so-called primary process mechanisms prevail in these organizations. But we cannot pursue this point here.

conviction, of feeling. Correspondingly, though objects are perceived and recognized they appear strange, and though thoughts are developed there is no conviction about them nor familiarity with them.[9] Bartlett (6) refers to this condition as follows: ". . . the mechanism of adult human memory demands an organization of 'schemata' depending upon an interplay of appetites, instincts, interests and ideals peculiar to any given subject. Thus if, as in some pathological cases, these active organizing sources of the 'schemata' get cut off from one another, the peculiar personal attributes of what is remembered fail to appear" (p. 212).

I could advance further strong evidence from psychopathology for the assumption of a cognitive organization around personal identity. For instance, I have demonstrated in my study and survey (86, 94) of alternating multiple personalities that the experiences acquired by such a person in one state are not, as a rule, available to cognition in his other state or states (see also Freud, 48, pp. 38–39). I could also advance further evidence (though it is rather weak) for this assumption by referring to the role of the identification figures in such projective tests as the T.A.T., and by reference to the relation between identity and memories in hypnotic age regression. Claparède's (24) "me-ness" (moiité) concept and the observations he based it on are certainly relevant, and so are some of the theoretical and experimental contributions on ego-involvement (4), as well as Koffka's (70) theory of the "core" of the memory trace, which — in contradistinction to the "shaft" of it — communicates with the "ego" and involves its "attitudes" in recall. However, none of these proves the point. "Personal identity" — as we know from E. Erikson's (31) studies[10] — reflects a complex and high-level integration of behavior which

---

[9] The experience of depersonalization is akin to the experience of something familiar in a strange context or in a stressful situation. Reports of examination experiences often contain examples of both. See p. 182 below.

[10] My equating of E. Erikson's identity concept with that of "personal identity" requires explanation. I hope that Erikson will soon publish the study of a case that has shed considerable light on the relationship of these two concepts.

is difficult to pin down when it works normally but which produces dramatic pathological effects when impaired.

I would like to mention two more points before we leave this observation.

The first relationship suggested by the three phases of this case of amnesia is the lack of a one-to-one relation between basic motivation and cognition. Comparing the three phases, the clinician would say that the controls that the personality exercises over drives are usually such that their interference with cognition is imperceptible and takes the form of individual proclivity. In the first phase a drive broke through these controls and interfered with the cognizing of all but its own representations. In the second phase the controls were reëstablished but — apparently as a precautionary measure — they became so widespread that they interfered extensively with cognition. In the third phase this excessive control was scaled down — it became limited to the drive itself — but, since the drive interfered with cognition in the first phase, its control could not but interfere with it too, and so it prevented the cognition of the experiences of the first phase. If we take this crude clinical description (crude this time in terms of clinical theory) at its face value, we note that there are yet other organizations — controls and defenses — to be taken into account here along with drive-organizations, since they too have a powerful regulating control over cognition (see Schafer, 96). Clinical observation attests to the great permanence of these controlling and defensive organizations. Indeed, the clinician is so impressed by their permanence that he refers to them as structures, and to their mode of function as mechanisms (49, 37).

Finally, a point about awareness or, as we usually refer to it, consciousness. In our usual state of consciousness we can become aware of our awareness. I assume that Bartlett (6) meant something similar when he spoke of the organism's ability "to turn round upon its own 'schemata'" (p. 208). In our three phases of amnesia we have three different forms of consciousness, which I characterized crudely as normal in the third phase, bewildered in the second, dazed in the first. Significantly enough, these gross characteristics are paralleled by the corresponding varieties of awareness of personal identity: in the third phase there is an awareness of identity with an unhampered potentiality to become aware of this fact; in the second phase there is a loss of awareness of personal identity with the awareness of this loss; in the first phase there is a loss of awareness of identity without awareness of this loss. Moreover, this constriction of awareness is paralleled by a progressive constriction of the range of feasible cognition.

The question arises whether the narrowing of consciousness is but an epiphenomenon accompanying the narrowing range of cognitions, or whether consciousness has a function of its own in normal as well as narrowed ranges of cognition. In either case it deserves to be taken out of limbo and to be restudied: in the first case as an index of the cognitive range, in the second as an organization subserving cognition. Indeed, clinical theory has been treating consciousness as an organization[11] through all the years in which most of experimental psychology used it as the generic term for deceptive and useless introspections. I hope that the observations I shall next present will lend support to the following theses: (1) consciousness can be usefully treated as an organization subserving cognition; (2) consciousness is not a unitary phenomenon but one that has a whole range of varieties, each corresponding to a different cognitive organization.

Before turning to these observations, however, I would like to quote Bartlett on the first point and Hebb on the second.

Bartlett (6) wrote: ". . . the organism discovers how to turn round upon its own 'schemata,' or, in other words, it becomes conscious" (p. 208); and ". . . one of the great functions of images in mental life . . . [is] to pick items out of 'schemata' and to rid the organism of overdetermination by the last preceding member of a given series. I would like to hold that this too could not occur except through the medium of consciousness. Again, I wish I knew precisely how it is brought about" (p. 209). "[This theory] . . . gives con-

---

[11] See Freud (38), chap. VII, particularly its last section; Silberer (104), also Rapaport (85) and (88), particularly the survey of the clinical conception of consciousness in my footnotes.

sciousness a definite function other than the mere fact of being aware" (p. 214). (See Oldfield and Zangwill, 78, both on Bartlett's more recent views and for a critique of these views.)

Hebb (58) accounts for the enduring organization of memory in terms of hypothetical closed neural circuits, which are organized into assemblies, which in turn are organized into phase sequences. He links consciousness to the degree of complexity of these memorial-conceptual cognitive organizations when he writes: "Consciousness then is to be identified theoretically with a certain degree of complexity of phase sequence in which both central and sensory facilitations merge . . ." (p. 145). This implies that consciousness is not an all-or-nothing phenomenon. Hebb spells it out: "The distinction is not between discrete and unrelated states, but between the extremes of a continuum" (p. 144).

It is worth noting that Bartlett, while attributing to consciousness a definite function besides awareness, speaks about it as a unitary phenomenon, while Hebb, seeing consciousness as a continuum of many variations, does not attribute any definite function to it.

The observation to which we now turn will, I hope, bring into relief a number of varieties of consciousness in addition to those discussed so far, and may make it plausible that the varieties of consciousness can, and probably should, be treated as relatively enduring organizations that perform definite functions.

III

This observation I take from a study in which I attempted night by night, over a prolonged period, to arouse myself after every thought-experience just enough to be able to record the experience and its content. The record contains thought-experiences ranging from dreams through intermediary forms like hypnogogic hallucinations, reveries, daydreams, to ordered waking thoughts.[12] I cannot discuss here the preparations for

---

[12] See Brenman (12), also Schafer (96). The examples mentioned here do not exhaust the varieties of cognitive experiences. For instance, they do not touch on the various forms of waking imagery, e.g. the form described by Hanawalt (56) and observed by me also, both in waking and reverie.

this recording, nor its precise conditions, nor even the many obvious and less obvious methodological pitfalls inherent in such a study (see Rapaport, 85).

At one point the record shows the following behavior. First, I had a dream, aroused myself after it, but could not "find" the dream. I made efforts to "capture" it. In the course of these efforts I noted that I was "slipping" into sleep again and told myself I must keep awake until I had "captured" and recorded the dream. Second, I did doze off and saw two "pin-waves" [13] approaching each other, at a small angle, in a dark sea, and made an effort to make them meet. Third, I fell asleep again and dreamed. The dream was: I am going to an examination at the University. I am . . . to be there . . . at eight. It is five . . . of eight and I am afraid I will be late . . . I arrive at the main door. The University is strange, it is not like my Alma Mater[14] . . . I do not know where to go . . . My fear that I will be late mounts . . . I ask the janitor . . . He begins to stutter in a most terrible way . . . I become more and more tense . . . I feel like bursting . . .(4) At this point the record of the dream broke off: I "fell off" and had a new experience. The record of this begins with a series of distorted words, some of which sound like Latin, others like Greek, Hebrew, or Arabic, followed by the comment: "I do not understand." This in turn is followed by: "A father in a monastery, panting, says to his son, 'I am so glad you got in before they shut the door.' "

I want to suggest that the four phases of this observation treat the same cognitive motif with different cognitive means, at different levels of awareness.[15] Such "translations" of

---

[13] "Pin-waves" is the word in the record. Actually the visual image was of two points progressing on straight lines at a small angle, leaving a very narrow wake behind them.

[14] The "strange"-ness of the University and the "it is not like my Alma Mater" were only "implicit" in the dream experience and only the recording brings them out explicitly. In other words, the knowledge that this *was* my Alma Mater and the fact that it did not look like my Alma Mater stood juxtaposed without being experienced as a contradiction.

[15] In the following, when I discuss these four different cognitive means by which the same motif is expressed in this observation, I will treat these observations only on the level of their *manifest form,* unless I specify otherwise.

thoughts from waking cognition into dream cognition have been observed by Freud (38) and others (103, 95, 77), from waking cognition into daydream cognition by Varendonck (109), from waking cognition into hypnogogic hallucinations by Silberer (105, 104) and others (50). My records contain examples of translation to and from a variety of distinguishable forms of cognition. The one I have chosen to present here contains the greatest number of translations of one theme in my records. May I add here that I transcribed all my records on the day following my taking them and, in doing so, I separately recorded additional observations as my memory supplied them.

The common cognitive motif of the four phases is set out in the first phase. It is the struggle to maintain consciousness until the dream is "captured"; but it also has the connotation[16] of a struggle between tired incapacity and ambition or duty. In other words, it is the antithesis: I must — I cannot.

The first phase I should like to describe as one of more or less waking consciousness and of waking cognition, which is, however, not particularly ordered and certainly not disciplined and logical. In the full waking state the experience of "slipping" is either absent or successfully countered by "effort," while my record of this phase shows that I felt I was waging a losing battle. However, I was aware of my slipping awareness, and, according to these records, such awareness of awareness appears to be a good criterion of the waking state. The thought content is that of waking cognition, in that it sets out the struggle with reasonable clarity, though it proposes no means of winning it, as ordered logical thought usually does in these records.

One more characteristic of this phase is noteworthy: I am aware of a "feel" of the lost dream and "reach" for it in my own thoughts: my consciousness turns back upon itself (see

---

By manifest form I mean what in the theory of dreams is called *manifest content* in contrast to *latent thought*.

[16] It is worth noting here that the waking cognition is not free of connotations though, as we shall see below, in comparison with other forms of cognition it appears to be.

Piaget, 82, also the mathematician Gonseth, 55). My "self," my own thoughts, my dream, my goal, my sleepiness, are all fairly well differentiated, even though my "reaching" for the dream is indistinct. Such differentiation too is, according to these records, a persistent characteristic of waking cognition in contradistinction to other forms of cognition. (See Lewin, 74, as well as Werner, 110, on differentiation in relation to the development of cognition; also Brenman, Gill, and Knight, 15, and Brenman, 14.)

The second phase I should like to describe as a hypnogogic hallucination of the sort Silberer (105) studied and described as a thought form characteristic of the transition from waking to sleep in which either the subjective state of the dozing-off person, or the pattern of his dozing-off thought, or the content of it is translated into imagery (see Isakower, 63). My records contain many of these. The most striking ones, like the one presented here, are related to the main obstacle to this sort of study — namely, the search for fading thought-experiences and the struggle against sleep — and take various forms: watching somebody trying to find a way out of a labyrinth; seeing somebody going towards a door only to discover that it is not a door but a shadow; following somebody's increasingly frantic approach towards a door as the door slowly shuts, and so on. Against this background one of the pin-waves of the second phase appears to represent my consciousness, the other the dream to be "captured." The small angle, implying that the meeting point is far away, and perhaps the "dark sea" too, translate the "feel" of a losing battle into this form of cognition.[17] The effort needs no translation.

What then are the characteristics of this state and this form of cognition? The cognition is first of all characterized by the predominance of visual imagery, absent in the first phase except for a vague directional image in "reaching" for the dream.[18] Indeed, my records indicate a progressive increase

[17] See E. Erikson (30) on the effect of the dream investigator's purpose on his dreams.

[18] See Buehler (22) for such directional images and note the relation of these observations to the "imageless thought" controversy.

of imagery from waking thought towards dream thought. This translation into images, however, also does away with the clear differentiations of the first phase: there is nothing here like the "turning back upon the dream" in the first phase. Dream and consciousness are leveled, equalized, both being represented by "pin-waves." [19] Yet some differentiation is still left: I myself am an observer of the scene and not a part of it as is usual in dreams. However, this self is a very peculiar observer, one who can make an effort to promote the process he is observing.

Here two further characteristics of the hypnogogic state emerge, one that it shares with daydreams and the other that it shares with dreams. My role, as an observer with a preserved awareness of personal identity and yet with the ability to influence the events, is characteristic of daydreams. The daydreamer can doctor up, interrupt, and restart his daydream[20] but while he, as the observer, retains awareness of his personal identity, he also usually appears as a figure in the daydream (109). The characteristic this hypnogogic hallucination shares with dreams is this: I, as an observer of the two "pin-waves," felt that I was exerting an effort to make them meet, but my ability to do so and the means by which I was doing so, remained unstated, or in other words, "implicit." Now, according to these records, "implicit knowledge" is characteristic of dreams and diminishes as waking thought is approached. For instance, in dreams one figure "knows" what the other figures feel, though nothing may be said and no expressive movement observed. I do not mean that we do not have such "implicit" cognitions in our waking state, but they are less frequent and we experience them with reservations as subjective impressions rather than with conviction as factual knowledge, or else we

[19] Concerning "leveling" compare (88), p. 625, footnote.

[20] There are people who at times do resume a dream that has been interrupted by their awakening. Some people at times do intend to dream about a definite theme and succeed in doing so. I have even encountered a few reports of dreams which the dreamer restarted and brought to an ending different from the original. But such "manipulations" are quite infrequent in dreams, while they are common in daydreams.

are called "psychic," or accused of projection. In dreams we rarely find such reservations and realize only on recording them, as I did, that what we "knew for certain" in the dream had no evidential grounds whatever. But then you may counter that you know psychologists whose "scientific beliefs" make them suspect of living in a continuous dream of this sort. With this I shall not take issue.

I must add here that in hypnogogic hallucinations the subject does not always remain an outside observer with a preserved awareness of personal identity. In those hypnogogic hallucinations in which the subject's personal identity is not preserved there are other features distinguishing the illusions from dreams.

The third phase will be readily recognized as a dream, even though I did not report its continuation for reasons of privacy.

The dream cognition of the common theme may be paraphrased as follows: I am trying to find the "test," and I am trying to pass the "test," but I am hampered by the unfamiliarity of what should be familiar and by "inarticulateness" (i.e. stuttering). This paraphrase shows that here the original theme has taken on additional connotations (see footnote, p. 162). But those familiar with the nature of dreams distinguish between manifest dream content and latent dream thought, and will recognize that this translation of the theme is merely a translation into the manifest dream content. If the theme has already picked up additional connotations in the manifest dream content, the latent dream thought adds further connotations, which expose the subjective meaning in my life pattern of the struggle between capacity and limitations on the one hand, duty and ambition on the other. Those familiar with dreams will also recognize that in this dream our common theme was used in the way day-residues of undischarged tension are usually used by dreams.

One of the salient characteristics of dream-cognition is, thus, that it takes its departure from day-residues of undischarged tension, and translates them into imagery that indicates, in an "implicit" fashion, the connotations of and place in the dreamer's scheme of life of the theme (i.e. day-residue) that has been translated.[21] This abundance of connotations in dream-cognition contrasts sharply with the waking cognitive function of the first phase, though people do use allusions and connotative designations in waking thought also. How does dream-cognition bring about these multiple connotations of its imagery? It does so by use of a variety of mechanisms (see Freud, 38, Werner, 110). It *condenses*, for example, when it represents in a single image "my Alma Mater," which the building definitely *is* to me in the dream, and a definitely strange building. It uses *displacement* and produces multiple images when it represents my "losing" the dream of the first phase — a dream which was mine and which I nevertheless did not know — on the one hand by my *unfamiliar* Alma Mater and on the other by the examination I *may not get to*. Moreover, it displaces or *projects* my tired incapacity and inarticulateness onto a stuttering janitor. It uses *substitutions* and *symbols* also, but I believe you will permit me to stop at this point.

These mechanisms are absent in the waking cognition of the first phase. While a detailed analysis of the second phase would show that they are present there, by and large the study of my records — and of dreams in general — indicates that the mechanisms illustrated here (as well as imagery and multiple connotations) are a predominant characteristic in dream-cognition, and diminish as we proceed through hypnogogic hallucination, reverie, and daydream toward waking cognition. Let me add that the form of awareness is also characteristic of the dream. In this dream I had no awareness of my personal identity and the awareness of the figure who represented me in the dream[22] appeared to be filled with the idea, "I must get

[21] See my commentary on Schroetter's (103), Roffenstein's (95) and Nachmansohn's (77) hypnotically suggested dreams. See also Poetzl (83) and Fisher (35, 36).

[22] I am referring to the figure "I" in the dream. Actually since the dream is a form of cognition, all the figures in it are the dreamer's thoughts and thus all represent him, or rather various aspects of his inner world. Lewis Carroll has put it thus: "He is dreaming now," said Tweedledee: "and what do you think he's dreaming about?" — Alice said: "Nobody can guess that." — "Why about you!" Tweedledee exclaimed . . . "And if he left off dreaming about you where do you suppose you'd be?" — "Where I am now, of course," said

there — I won't," much as our amnesia patient was with his
"I must end it all" in the first phase of his illness. While there
are dreams during which some awareness of one's personal
identity is represented by the feeling and thought that "this
is just a dream," they are the exception rather than the rule,
both in records of my dreams and in other people's dreams
which I have collected.

Finally, let me mention that my questioning of the janitor
and his stuttering were only "implicit" (see above, p. 170)
in the dream. I "knew" that I asked and that he "stut-
tered" in answer, but there were no words. I have indicated
before that this "implicitness" is characteristic of dream-cognition and diminishes as waking thought is approached.

In general, a multitude of connotations — usually merci-
fully hidden from our waking cognition by defensive and controlling organizations — are "recruited" (to use Hebb's term)
to the dream-theme by dream-cognition. Dream-cognition
achieves this "recruitment" — which enriches, as it were, the
themes of our waking thought — by means of mechanisms that
in other forms of cognition are more or less proscribed. The
free use of these mechanisms is characteristic of dream-cognition, which shares it only with symptom-forming processes and
with psychotic thought-disorders (see Freud, 44, 45). Yet all
cognitive forms make some use of or show some intrusion of
these mechanisms. For example, they are obviously used in
poetry and in the arts in general (see Empson, 26, Brooks, 19,
and Kris, 72).

Let us now turn to the fourth phase of our observation. I
shall call it a reverie.[23] The term "reverie" is often used as a
synonym for daydream. I, however, shall use it to mean a state

---

Alice. — "Not you!" Tweedledee retorted contemptuously. "*You'd be no-
where. Why, you're only a sort of thing in his dream!*" [Italics mine.] — "If
that there King was to wake," added Tweedledum, "you'd go out — bang! —
just like a candle!" "I shouldn't!" Alice exclaimed indignantly. "Besides, if
I'm only a sort of thing in his dream, what are *you* . . . ?" "Ditto," said
Tweedledum. — "Ditto, ditto!" cried Tweedledee. [*Through the Looking-
Glass.*]

[23] For a survey of a variety of kindred phenomena see Brenman (12). Freud
(38) also noted a variety of "dream" that is akin to these.

of consciousness and a form of cognition midway between those of daydream and hypnogogic hallucination. I hope that the discussion that follows here will justify this distinction.

I would like to suggest that the reverie of this fourth phase translates our theme to the form of a wish-fulfillment. The father's words, "I am so glad that you got in before they shut the door," as well as the fact that he says this, "panting," implies that there *was* a question — "Will he get in, or will he not?" — which is our theme. But this form of cognition places the struggle in the past and makes the present a "happy ending." This aspect of reverie-cognition is akin to the wish-fulfillment of daydreams (109). Who of us has not fancied a glorious reception by his teacher, beloved, or parent, after some equally fancied great deed? This very feature is one of the distinctions between reverie-cognition and dream-cognition. In the latter, past and future are expressed only by "implication" (38, 106). What are the other characteristics that distinguish reverie-cognition from dream-cognition? To answer this question I must explain a bit further the reverie of the fourth phase. In this cognitive experience, as in phase two, I was an observer. I *heard* the distorted words; I *saw* the monastery with a chain across the gate; then I *saw* the father speaking to the son and panting. But it was *I* who interjected after the distorted words: "I don't understand." The facts that I, as a person, was outside the scene and made a comment, and the explicit presence of verbalization, distinguish this fourth phase from dream-cognition.[24] My records show that as one progresses from waking to dream-cognition the use of verbalization decreases. Not that there is *no* explicit verbalization in dreams, but it is rare, and, as a rule, it is a repetition of a familiar or recently heard phrase, as Freud (38) noted.

Let us note that this reverie arose when, in the course of recording the dream of the third phase, I reached the stuttering of the janitor and — as my supplementary record shows — I

---

[24] There are also dreams in which the person representing the dreamer is on the sidelines as a mere observer. While this is not quite the same as the reverie observer's role, it does point up that these distinguishing characteristics refer to differences in frequency and are not qualitative all-or-nothing distinctions.

again experienced, while recording, the mounting tension. It appears that the distorted words translate into reverie-cognition the janitor's stuttering — which, to put it colloquially, was "all Greek to me" — as well as my inability to capture the lost dream of the first phase. Moreover, it appears that the reëxperienced tension was translated into the dream by the "panting" of the father.

However, the reverie-cognition also shows features that contrast sharply with the waking cognition of the first phase and are akin to those of the dream. The abundance of visual imagery is obviously one of these features, the connotative-recruiting is another. The appearance of the father, of the monastery, and of the "they" who shut the doors, is the most obvious set of features of this sort, locating the meaning of the struggle of capacity and inability with duty and ambition, in the pattern of my life. The details of the visual imagery imply further connotations and reveal the mechanisms by which the recruiting and multiple connotations were brought about. I shall not dwell on these here.

While we have always known that in general we can distinguish our thoughts, daydreams, and dreams from each other, I hope I have demonstrated that these as well as other forms of cognition can be distinguished from each other by objective criteria.[25] The criteria that I found were: use of visual imagery, use of verbalization, awareness of awareness (implying the ability to turn round upon the content or state of consciousness), explicitness versus implicitness, differentiation, recruiting connotative enrichment by means of the mechanisms of condensation, displacement, and so on. There are still others to which I could not refer in this brief compass without recourse to clinical terminology and theory.[26]

In connection with the dream of the third phase, I have referred to controlling and defensive organizations, but I have

[25] These criteria, as indicated before, are not qualitative distinctions, but rather quantitative parameters.

[26] Psychoanalytic theory subsumes these criteria under the generic concept "primary process" to distinguish them from the criteria of the goal-directed, ordered, and logical forms of thought, which in turn are subsumed under the generic concept "secondary process" (see 38, chap. VII, and 88, pt. VII).

refrained from discussing motivations. The motivations involved here range from high-level derivative motivations, such as duty, to basic drives. Our compass, the conceptual means to which I have limited myself here, and — last but not least — personal considerations, prevent me from entering upon these.

I feel that this demonstration of a variety of distinguishable forms of cognition — if sustained by further observations — is a demonstration of cognitive organizations other than those I discussed in my introduction and in the first observation I presented. These cognitive organizations, just like those involved in the three phases of the case of amnesia, are accompanied by varieties of awareness (that is, consciousness) that appear to be specific to them (see p. 162). This suggests that varieties of consciousness are themselves organized means of cognition.[27] It also seems to support the contention that we are dealing here with quasi-stable cognitive organizations that use[28] different tools or mechanisms of cognition, and are themselves organized means of cognition.

[27] I cannot pursue this point here. A further demonstration that it is advantageous to treat varieties of consciousness not as epiphenomena of cognition, but rather as cognitive organizations integrating certain cognitive forms, would require the conceptual means of clinical (psychoanalytic) theory. See Rapaport (85).

[28] Here, as elsewhere in this paper, the term "use" requires some clarification. I am indebted to Dr. George Klein for pointing this out to me. What I mean is that the assemblies of cognitive forms (here called tools) are not random, but rather constitute a cohesive quasi-stable organization (here called cognitive organization). In this sense there is no justification for the term "use." The relationship in question is that of the whole to its parts and vice versa: the whole *is* the relationship system of its parts and the parts are defined by their place in the whole. To spell this out concretely: we recognize a cognitive organization by the cognitive forms used, and the significance of any single cognitive form (since it can appear in many cognitive organizations) derives from the cognitive organization within which it appears. But there *is* a sense in which the term "use" is justified. The cognitive organizations give form to contents that in turn express the motivations, intentions, etc., of the organism. The cognitive forms (tools) may therefore be said to be *used* in this form-giving and -expressing process. Dr. George Klein raises the further question: "Who uses whom?" Indeed there are observations necessitating the assumption that this "utilization" process can also work in the reverse direction. This, however, leads to the complex problems to which Allport's (4) concept of "functional autonomy" and Hartmann's (57) concept "ego autonomy" refer, and these I cannot pursue further here.

IV

Now I shall turn to some observations on certain forms of schizophrenic pathology of thought. I am taking these partly from our studies in diagnostic testing (93, vol. II) and partly from observations of pathology of thought in the course of psychotherapy. (See 9, 10, 11, my footnote commentary on them in 88, and also Kasanin, 65.)

I presented the first observation, on amnesia, to illustrate some cognitive organizations — which subserve the integration of cognition — laid bare, as it were, by pathology. I presented the second observation to demonstrate some further cognitive organizations, characteristic of special states such as dreams, reveries, and so on. In the examples to follow, I should like to spotlight other cognitive organizations by focusing on the forms of cognition that arise when the schizophrenic process disrupts such organizations so that their integrative function fails.

Observation A. Schizophrenic patients reporting their dreams comment at times: "When I awoke I was not sure whether I dreamed it or it really did happen." At other times they report: "As I woke up this morning, for a while I was uncertain whether I was awake or dreaming."

Observation B. 1. A schizophrenic patient's response to the seventh Rorschach card is: "Six sharks." The examiner inquires: "What makes it look like that?" The patient's answer: "Because yesterday I read 'The Raft.' "

2. A schizophrenic patient's response to the first Rorschach card: "A histological plate." Inquiry: "What makes it look like that?" Answer: "The sensation obtaining between light and one's eyes."

3. A schizophrenic patient's response to a part of the sixth Rorschach card: "A vaginal smear containing gonococci." Inquiry: "What makes it look like that?" Answer: "The ink makes it look like that."

Observation C. A young schizophrenic patient describes to his therapist a conversation with another young patient, in relation to whom he displays a variety of feelings, ideas, and impulses which he cannot consciously admit in relation to his therapist. The conversation is the last· of a series of similar ones. The patient tells the other patient that he feels intellectually inferior, indeed he thinks he may be a moron. The other obligingly agrees. Our patient now — as in earlier conversations — suddenly experiences the other's words as gospel truth, and indeed as his own thought and conviction. All he can and does ask from the other is: "How did you find it out?" The other again obliges, saying that he heard it from his therapist, who is the friend of our patient's therapist, who had heard it from our patient. Our patient experiences this also as "true." But at this point suddenly something dramatic happened which the patient recounted as follows: "I saw you telling his therapist that I am a moron, and in the moment I saw you I *knew* that this was not my thought but something I just heard, something he tried to put over on me, something that was not true."

First, let me state that none of these observations is exceptional or unique in the clinician's experience (see Arieti, 5, and note, p. 167) or in my records. Secondly, I would like to suggest that all these observations have in common one feature that may be crudely characterized as pertaining to an impairment of a "frame of reference" or of its use. I choose the term "frame of reference" here only because it is well-worn (for a different interpretation, see Helson, 60, particularly pp. 379 ff.). Otherwise, however, it is a catch-all whose contents are heterogeneous and will have to be sorted out sooner or later. Most cognitive organizations have at one time or another been referred to as "frames of reference."

In Observation A, the "frames of reference" of *waking* and *dreaming* cognition blur. In Observation C, the "frames of reference" of that which is cognized as *"only a thought"* and of that which is cognized as *true* shade into each other. In each of the three B Observations, the psychological-perceptual "frame of reference" is left for another one, which in B 1 is the psychological-memorial, in B 2 the physiological-perceptual, and in B 3 the realistic-artifactual "frame of reference." I shall explain these terms later.

Let us take these observations one by one.

Observation A implies that in schizophrenic pathology dreams may appear to be waking experiences and waking experiences may appear to be dreams. It is no explanation to say simply that the discrimination between waking- and dream-cognition fails here because the schizophrenic's experience is dreamlike anyway; *first,* because it restates rather than explains the phenomenon; *second,* because the expression "the schizophrenic's experience is dreamlike" is a meaningless generality; *third,* because the very patients who report such experiences have dreams which they can discriminate from waking, and the very fact of their report — that is, their awareness of this — shows not an absence but a blurring of discrimination between waking- and dream-cognition.

But what is it in these experiences that can and has to be discriminated — is it their cognitive contents or is it something else? I attempted to demonstrate above by comparing the translations of a single theme into the "language" of four different cognitive organizations that dream-cognition, waking-cognition, and so on, are distinguishable and cohesive cognitive organizations. This might suggest that the different contents, through which the common theme is expressed in the various cognitive organizations, are the means by which we distinguish these organizations. Therefore, let me present an example in which the manifest cognitive content is the same both in waking- and in dream-cognition, though the theme it represents may be different in each.[29] A young male patient reports two experiences: in the first experience he fell asleep with the light on and saw a bus boy come to his room, but afterwards he could not recall whether he actually woke up and saw the bus boy come in or whether he dreamed it. In the second experience he was more certain that he was actually asleep and dreamed that he was awake and saw the bus boy walk into his room. The content of these two experiences is identical and indistinguishable from waking experience. The first experience is to be compared not only with the second more or less definite dream experience, but also with those dreams, familiar to

[29] I borrow this example from Dr. Peter Wolff.

the clinician, whose manifest content is indistinguishable from an actual and repeated experience of the subject, who nevertheless readily recognizes it as a dream. Thus it seems that what can be and is to be identified as waking- or dream-cognition is not the cognitive content but something that transcends the content. This does not prove, but may lend further plausibility to, the contention that dream-cognition and waking-cognition each forms subjectively and objectively distinguishable cohesive cognitive organizations.

How does this observation relate to normal phenomena?

First of all, neurotic and "normal" people also have such experiences. Some of us always arise with a dreamy feeling, others carry the moods and affects of their dreams into the waking state, and yet others experience the uncertainty: "Was it really just a dream?" But unlike the schizophrenic's uncertainty, ours is passing and is either characterologically anchored so that we are accustomed to it and not alarmed by it, or else it is related to particularly intense motivations.[30]

Secondly, the question arises, how do we usually distinguish our dream experience from a waking one? We do have dreams that seem to us to be entirely real, but these are rare and usually arouse us from our sleep. We also have dreams during which we can "tell" ourselves that "this is just a dream." [31] In these we retain to some extent the awareness of our personal identity and our role as the observer of the scene. Such dreams are rare, however. Usually the distinction between dream and waking experience is far subtler: as a rule we experience the dream, while we are dreaming it, as a reality in which we participate, and yet we experience it with a "belief of reality" (see Freud, 43, Rapaport, 89) different from that which characterizes waking-cognition. This subtle difference

[30] An example: a young man — who was not a psychiatric patient either before or after this incident of many years ago — made a "clean break" with a girl-friend. The night following this event he "saw" the girl standing at his bedside and shouted at her, "I told you. You must not come here again." Throughout the experience he felt he was awake and only when roused to full waking by his own voice did he realize the nature of his experience.

[31] A rather complicated variant of this is the dream in which the content of the subject's dream is that he is dreaming.

appears to be of the same order as the difference between visual memory images and the visual images in daydreams. Visual memory images contain many[32] of the spatial, temporal, and personal relationships of the contents that are cognized through them, while the visual images of daydreams tend to contain fewer or none at all.[33] All of us have had images of the "castle in Spain," or "the prancing steed," which, unlike memory images, carried no indications of their origins. You may also remember the strangeness of some of the images aroused in you by "La Belle Dame Sans Merci," or "Kubla Khan." The process that strips visual memory images of their relational (spatial, temporal, personal) characteristics and turns them into the visual images of imagination is probably similar to that which turns the contents of personal experience into the sort of impersonal information that intelligence tests measure.[34] Be that as it may, the "belief of reality" of waking-cognition seems to depend partly on the availability of spatial,

---

[32] Such relationships have been conceptualized variously in terms of schemata (6), recruitment (58), as well as in terms of registration in various memory systems (38). See also Schafer (97).

[33] This is not a hard-and-fast distinction. Daydreams too may have visual images rich in memorial connotations.

[34] There is a parallel here also to the relation between deliberate problem-solving behavior and habituated motor behavior. Hartmann's (57) "automatization" concept appears relevant to these relationships. A perceptual image, upon having been perceived, enters a variety of relations and its content is thereby enriched. The full memorial image is in this sense rich in characteristics. These very relationships, however, also exert a selective effect on the raw material of *perception,* and lay the groundwork for transforming it into a concept that is impoverished in characteristics. Both the enrichment and the impoverishment processes begin with these relationships. The product of the first is the memory laden with the relational characteristics of the experience, as well as with those of prior and subsequent related experiences; the memories the therapist deals with tend to be of this sort. The product of the second is the *concept* held generally and divested of the relational earmarks of its origin. Knowledge, and information in general, is an intermediary station — albeit frequently a final stop for many — on the way to the concept. Hebb (58) describes concept-formation in a manner which is, to my mind, analogous with the one described here. The question may arise how it is that daydream and dream images, which are so laden with personal relevance, are characterized here as "impoverished." Actually it is the impoverishment in memorial-relational characteristics that makes the image amenable to the process that lends it multiple connotations (see pp. 175–176 above). As a rule, only the day-residues of the dream retain their relational characteristics.

temporal, and similar characteristics and partly on a type of consciousness — awareness of awareness — which if necessary can turn round on these characteristics, and these may well be the factors that distinguish the "belief of reality" of the waking state from that of dream-cognition. Let us remember that we usually become aware of the multiple connotations of dream-cognition only when we turn round upon the dream in the subsequent waking state, equipped with the technique of dream interpretation.

The clinician subsumes the distinctions here discussed under the heading of reality testing (see Freud, 41). But to academic psychology also, these distinctions are familiar from Brentano's act-psychology (16, 17, 18, 75), according to which the organism is not passive in its cognitive experiences, and therefore the cognitive *act* is to be distinguished and studied apart from the cognitive *content*. The cognitive act was termed "intention" by Brentano. Perception, thought, imagination, and so on, may all have the same cognitive content, yet their intentional act is different. Generalizing from Brentano's view, we might say that we can "intend" a table by perceptual, memorial, conceptual, hallucinatory, or dream intentions (see Rapaport, 89, 88). These differences in intention will then be assumed to lend, or will fail to lend, or will lend a certain quality of "belief of reality" to the cognized content. It goes without saying that most of these distinctions are readily made by us in subjective experience; but it also should go without saying that these distinctions are indispensable tools for orientation in reality. Perceptual intentions distinguish objects that are present from absent ones, which cannot be perceptually intended. Perceptual intention, therefore, indicates that the object is present and can be approached by a more or less direct route. Other kinds of intentions are no less important: they make it possible to intend the absent object and to discover its memorial-historical, contextual, and conceptual relations, and thereby enable us to find these objects in reality by way of a detour (see Freud, 38, chap. VII, Schilder, 100, 101, Rapaport, 92, 87).

It seems feasible to define the concept of intention so as to

make it independent of its act-psychological trappings and to
link certain varieties of intent with certain cognitive organizations. Our discrimination between the seen and the dreamed,
the remembered and the imagined, is so stable that it would
seem to be more justifiable to assume that this stability is
vouchsafed by relatively stable cognitive organizations and
intentions pertaining to them, than to assume that this stability
is achieved by *ad hoc* discriminatory judgments made from
occasion to occasion (102, 92).

Let me now turn to Observation B.[35] Our interest in each
of the three examples centers on the patient's answer to the
Rorschach-test inquiry. Most subjects (including patients)
have a common understanding of the standard inquiry, "What
makes it look like that?" as shown by the fact that they respond to it within the same "frame of reference." I will call it
here the *psychological-perceptual frame of reference*. Let me
illustrate. Take the response: "A bat." Inquiry: "What makes
it look like that?" Answer: "It impressed me as a bat because
it had two wings, a body, a head with big ears, and its color
was dark gray." This is an explanation in psychological terms
since the subject speaks about his impressions and not about
unequivocal facts of reality; moreover, it is also an explanation
in perceptual terms since he indicates the features that gave
rise to his impression. The question with which the Rorschach
cards are presented is also within this "frame of reference":
"What does this look like to you?" It asks for a subjective yet
still perceptual impression. Subjects vary in their comprehen-
sion of the question, as shown by the fact that the responses of
some stress the subjective side, those of others the perceptual
side. The former tend to give their impressions freely, the latter tend to search for what the inkblot "really represents."
These differences of style show intraindividual consistency and
have considerable importance in diagnosing personality organization (93, vol. II).

---

[35] These examples are taken from Rapaport, Schafer, Gill (93) vol. II,
Appendix II, which contains the full collation of such "deviant verbalizations"
of the patient population discussed in the volume. See also pp. 324–365 of the
volume.

Let us now see how our schizophrenic patients understood the inquiry. In the first example (see Benjamin, 7) the patient's explanation of his "six sharks" is: "Because yesterday I read 'The Raft.' " Is this a psychological-perceptual explanation? It is a psychological explanation, that is, one in terms of subjective experience, but this subjective experience is in terms of memory rather than perception. While inquiry in terms of the psychological-perceptual "frame of reference" tends to bring forth answers within the same "frame of reference," our patient's answer shifted to the psychological-memorial "frame of reference."

A similar shift occurs in the second example (see Goldstein, 54, and Cameron, 23). The patient explains his "histological plate" by "the sensation obtaining between the light and one's eyes." True, without the impact of the light no response to the card could have taken place. But is this a psychological-perceptual explanation? It has something to do with the perceptual, namely, with its physics and physiology, but it contains no trace of the psychologically subjective. The patient shifted from the psychological-perceptual frame of reference of the inquiry to the physiological-perceptual frame of reference of the answer.

The shift in the third example (see above) is in the same direction as the second, only more extreme. The patient explains the "vaginal smear containing gonococci" by "the ink makes it look like that." Again there is no trace of the psychologically subjective in the explanation. It seems to pertain to the "objective cause" of perception, and reflects what as a philosophy would pass as "naïve realism." It could well have come from Piaget's (81, 79) collection of causal explanations taken from that phase of the child's development which Piaget calls "artificialistic," and in which things happen or are the way they are because they were made by someone to happen or to be that way. Thus, this patient shifted from the psychological-perceptual "frame of reference" to the realistic-artifactual.

I have pointed out that within the psychological-perceptual frame of reference there is room for a wide variety of styles.

These patients, however, overstep this frame of reference: the first one does so in the subjective-psychological direction, disregarding perception, while the second and third do so in the perceptual direction; losing sight of their subjectivity, they take their perceptions for objective truth. In these excesses they seem like caricatures of philosophers: the first one a caricature of the idealist-rationalist, the latter two of the pragmatic naïve realist. Psychologists of various beliefs and some sense of humor will discover their own caricatures in these patients. But this comparison should not mislead us: philosophical systems are complex cognitive organizations of high order (see Piaget, 82, Erikson, 31), showing great qualitative and quantitative differences in interindividual distribution, while the "frames of reference" I discuss here are ubiquitous and, from the beginning of adolescence, belong to our basic psychological equipment.

These are only a few examples of the many fixed "frames of reference" that orient us to the appropriate level of discourse and abstraction and keep us from changing our "realm of discourse." Orientation in our multilayered world of reality would seem rather hopeless without the steering of "frames of reference." Most schizophrenic and many obsessional patients lack this automatic steering. Their attempts to decide from occasion to occasion the level of discourse in which to move results either in shifts of the sort we have seen or in an inability to make a shift when it is appropriate,[36] or in a state of hopeless confusion. Such observations prompt the clinician to attribute structure character to these frames of reference. Problem-solving research is familiar with the normal effects of frames of reference that permit no shifting and hold the subject in a vise, as well as with those that do not compel any persistence (see Woodworth, 111, chaps. XXIX and XXX, Duncker, 25).

I have already indicated that inquiries made in a psychological-perceptual frame of reference draw answers within the same frame of reference. Elsewhere (93, 88) I have discussed the grounds for considering that relationships of the question-

---

[36] See Benjamin (7). See also Scheerer (98); many of the considerations advanced in this paper have a close affinity to his point of view.

answer variety are mediated by anticipations. I have also
pointed out that many such anticipations are structurally
guaranteed by linguistic forms, such as conjunctions (but,
though, and so on). It seems to me that there is a close relation
between anticipations and the type of "frame of reference" I
have discussed here. Discourse seems to proceed by ever-nar-
rowing anticipations and these "frames of reference" seem to
form early steps in this narrowing course, while the anticipations that are anchored in specific linguistic forms are later
ones.

May I stress that I chose these three examples illustrating
"frames of reference" for the simplicity with which they could
be presented, and labeled them *ad hoc*.[37] There is no reason
to assume that they or their malfunctions are any more or any
less important than the many other frames of reference we use,
and the malfunctions of which we observe every day. Much —
though by no means all — of what the Wurzburg School (2,
108) termed "Einstellung" and "Bewusstseinslage," as well as
what J. Gibson (52) calls "set," and G. Allport (3) calls "attitude" (particularly instrumental attitude), show pathological
malfunctions similar to those of "frames of reference," and
there are reasons to believe that they could be conceptualized
as "frames of reference" in the sense of the term used here.

Let us now turn to Observation C, concerning the patient
who experienced the thoughts of another first as "true" and
his own, and then suddenly discovered their real nature.
If we were to rank the cognitive organizations dealt with in
this section, the "frames of reference" would seem the most
narrow and specific ones, those related to waking- versus
dream-cognition broader and more general, and the ones we
are about to discuss the broadest and most general, and of the
same order as the cognitive organization centering around personal identity discussed in the observation on amnesia. The
pathology in the present example is related to depersonalization, which we mentioned in the same connection.

[37] Dr. George Klein suggests — and I agree — that the specific "frames of
reference" treated here might well have been discussed in Heider's (59) terms of
"thing" and "medium," since they deal with the mediation of the "thing character" of the object.

On first inspection, our patient's pathology seems to be his lack of discrimination between "This I heard," and "This is what I think," and between "It occurred to me," and "It is true." This at first appears to be an impairment of frames of reference. Indeed, the shift from "This I heard" to "This is what I think" is a shift from the hearsay-perceptual to the judging-cognitive "frame of reference"; and the shift from "It occurred to me" to "It is true," a shift from the freely wandering-cognitive to the veridical-cognitive "frame of reference." May I stress again that these are *ad hoc* labels.

But there is more to this than just an impairment of "frame of reference." These shifts in "frame of reference" differ from those of the Rorschach inquiries: their net effect is to leave the subject open to and at the mercy of the ideas of others, as well as of his own. In clinical parlance, this impairment of "frames of reference" amounts to a weakening of the boundary between the person and his environment. The clinician's retrospective reconstruction (41, 46, 99), as well as Piaget's direct observations, suggests that an indistinctness of this boundary is characteristic of early phases of individual development. Moreover, H. Werner (110) has shown that some weakness — either circumscribed or general — of the boundary between the person and his environment is widespread both in developmental and pathological forms. Indeed, there seems to be a consensus that some weakness or modification of this boundary is one of the underlying ingredients of magical and animistic beliefs and practices (see Levy-Bruehl, 73, Freud, 42, Piaget, 80).

It seems then that in this observation the impairment of the frame of reference involves the impairment of that higher-order integration represented by the boundary between that which belongs to the person and that which does not. The circumstances under which integration was restored tend to corroborate this and also tend to connect this higher-order integration with that cognitive organization centered around personal identity which we discussed in connection with the second phase of amnesia. To make this plausible, I have to enter into clinical considerations. The patient in question has not lost awareness of personal identity as our amnesia patient had. He "knows" who he is. He has lost personal identity only in the sense of depersonalization (see Schilder, 102, pp. 304 ff., and for further sources see my footnotes to the same pages). This depersonalization was a creeping and partial one of which he was scarcely aware before therapy. The patient's failure to distinguish "hearsay" from "thought," and so on, was accordingly also only partial: it was limited to contact with people with whom he formed powerful identifications (see Freud, 47, 48). Indeed, to consider the other's thoughts as "true" and one's own is one aspect of the early phase of any strong identification. Such identifications were sought by our patient in an effort to find a substitute for his personal identity, and as a building-stone towards a "new identity." Identity is an integrate of identifications (see Erikson, 31, Freud, 48). Dysfunction of personal identity, as in our case of amnesia, as well as its substitution by a single intensive identification, interfere with cognition just as the substitution of a single author's system for the whole of psychology interferes with psychological understanding (see Freud, 48, pp. 38–39).

I have mentioned that our patient displayed towards the other patient a variety of ideas and impulses which he could not use in relation to his therapist. This both facilitated and hampered his identification with the therapist. But when the therapist's image arose in his mind he suddenly "discovered" a frame of reference other than that of the identification with the other patient, and in this frame of reference he recognized the "hearsay" for what it was.[38] Indeed, he later used the therapist's image as a magic device to help him distinguish "hearsay" from "own thought," as well as "thought" from "truth." It will be no surprise to you to learn that he also experienced the same difficulties in relation to his therapist. In both cases intensive single identifications usurped the function of identity and left the patient's cognition open and vulnerable

[38] It is implied that the appearance of the therapist's image was related to the patient's identification with him and that forming this identification was part of the patient's work at reconstituting his identity. It is this background that underlay the effectiveness of the therapist's image in mobilizing the "frame of reference" which had been in abeyance.

in relation to the cognitions of the person with whom he identified.

If you consider that the great achievement of organisms is their relative independence from their environment, then the significance of the integrative organization, and of its impairment, comes into full relief. But the independence from their environment achieved by "open systems" — to use Bertalanffy's (8) term — is always relative. Similarly, the effectiveness of the integration of cognitions in terms of personal identity, which delineates the person from his environment, is also only relative. I have already indicated that in the widespread magical and animistic beliefs and practices this integration and delineation is fluid. But there are other normal forms that also demonstrate the relativity of this integration. I shall not dwell on the multitude of pertinent hypnotic phenomena and will refer you simply to the studies of Gill and Brenman (13, 15). Nor will I discuss the consequences for cognition of the state of "being in love" — they are well known. I should like to mention only that "gullibility" is in many cases — though certainly not in all — a normal and enduring counterpart of the pathological gullibility of our patient. Moreover, when cognition ventures into areas where tested knowledge is meager, or into areas in which the person's information is slight, normal dysfunction akin to this pathology crops up readily.

V

Throughout this paper I have centered on relatively enduring forms in contrast to passing processes. I have suggested that we need concepts of organization- or structure-character to account for all these quasi-stable enduring forms. I am not sure but what the troubles of learning theory are due to its failure — cognitive maps, and habit-hierarchies to the contrary notwithstanding — to recognize the multitude and variety of these enduring forms. But this criticism may not be fair, and learning theories may simply be reluctant to accord a conceptual status to these relatively enduring forms, on the assumption that these can and must be reduced to a few simple constructs, even if reduction takes a long time. However, the relation of this persistent reducing to the lure of "the psychology of the empty organism" is patent.

My stress upon relatively enduring organization parallels a change of emphasis in psychoanalytic theory. The clearest expression of this change is the development of psychoanalytic ego-psychology in the last thirty years. Early psychoanalysis laid great stress upon motivations and their gratification processes. Indeed it may be considered the pioneer of the motivational point of view among psychologies. The development of ego-psychology *added* an equal stress upon the relatively enduring organizations that not only subserve the defense against and control of these motivations but may give rise to new motivations and may also subserve the adaptation of the organism to its environment. It seems that with this stress on relatively enduring controlling- and means-organzations, psychoanalytic psychology finds itself again in a pioneering role.

The specific cognitive organizations or structures that I discussed were meant only as illustrations. My study of these is still in the initial stage and I hold no brief for them, except insofar as they illustrate my general point. Nor for that matter do I hold a brief for any specific psychoanalytic concept that refers to relatively enduring structures. Further study may well replace these concepts. But it cannot abolish the phenomena to which the present structure-concepts refer. So far psychoanalysis is the only theory that has attempted to take account of these phenomena. If this theory is weak by the yardstick of academic psychology, the latter has not yet proposed a better one to account for these phenomena and the poet's words may well apply: "Whither we cannot fly, we go limping; the Scripture saith, limping is no sin." [39]

BIBLIOGRAPHY

1. Abeles, M., and P. Schilder. Psychogenetic loss of personal identity: amnesia. *Arch. Neurol. Psychiat.*, 34:587–604 (1935).
2. Ach, N. *Ueber die Willenstaetigkeit und das Denken.* Goettingen, Vandenhoeck und Ruprecht (1905).

[39] Rueckert: Die Makamen des Hariri (Freud quoted these lines in his "Beyond the Pleasure Principle").

3. Allport, G. "Attitudes." In Murchison, Carl (ed.), *A Handbook of Social Psychology*. Worcester: Clark Univ. Press (1935).
4. Allport, G. *The Nature of Personality: Selected Papers*. Cambridge: Addison-Wesley (1950).
5. Arieti, S. *Interpretation of Schizophrenia*. New York: Brunner (1955).
6. Bartlett, F. C. *Remembering: A Study in Experimental and Social Psychology*. Cambridge, England: Cambridge Univ. Press (1932).
7. Benjamin, J. "A method for distinguishing and evaluating formal thinking disorders in schizophrenia." In (65), pp. 65–90.
8. Bertalanffy, L. The theory of open systems in physics and biology. *Science*, 111:23–30 (1950).
9. Bleuler, E. "Autistic thinking." In (88), pp. 399–437.
10. Bleuler, E. "Autistic-undisciplined thinking." In (88), pp. 438–450.
11. Bleuler, E. "The basic symptoms of schizophrenia." In (88), pp. 581–649.
12. Brenman, M. Dreams and hypnosis. *Psa. Quart.*, 18:455–465 (1949).
13. Brenman, M., M. Gill, and F. Hacker. Alterations in the state of the ego in hypnosis. *Bull. Menninger Clin.*, 11:60–66 (1947).
14. Brenman, M. "The phenomena of hypnosis." In *Problems of Consciousness*, Transactions of the First Conference. New York: Josiah Macy, Jr., Foundation (1951), pp. 123–163.
15. Brenman, M., M. Gill, and R. P. Knight. Spontaneous fluctuations in depth of hypnosis and their implications for ego-function. *Int. J. Psa.*, 33:22–33 (1952).
16. Brentano, F. *Psychologie vom empirischen Standpunkt*. Leipzig: Dunker and Humbolt (1874).
17. Brentano, F. *Vom sinnlichen und noetischen Bewusstsein*. Leipzig: Felix Meiner (1928).
18. Brentano, F. *Von der Klassifikation der psychischen Phaenomene*. Leipzig: Dunker and Humbolt (1911).
19. Brooks, C. *Modern Poetry and the Tradition*. Chapel Hill: Univ. of North Carolina Press (1939).
20. Bruner, J., and L. Postman. Tension and tension release as organizing factors in perception. *J. Pers.*, 15:300–308 (1947).
21. Bruner, J., and C. Goodman. Value and need as organizing factors in perception. *J. Abn. Soc. Psychol.*, 42:33–44 (1947).
22. Buehler, K. "On thought connections." In (88), pp. 39–57.
23. Cameron, N. "Experimental analysis of schizophrenic thinking." In (65), pp. 50–64.
24. Claparède, E. "Recognition and 'me-ness.'" In (88), pp. 58–75.
25. Duncker, K. *The Structure and Dynamics of Problem-Solving Processes*. Washington: American Psychological Association (1945).
26. Empson, W. *Seven Types of Ambiguity*. Rev. ed. Norfolk, Conn.: New Directions (1949).

27. Erickson, M. Experimental demonstration of the psychopathology of everyday life. *Psa. Quart.*, 8:338–353 (1939).

28. Erickson, M., and E. Erickson. Concerning the nature and character of post-hypnotic behavior. *J. General Psychol.*, 24:95–133 (1941).

29. Erikson, E. *Childhood and Society*. New York: Norton (1950).

30. Erikson, E. The dream specimen of psychoanalysis. *J. Amer. Psa. Assoc.*, 2:5–56 (1954).

31. Erikson, E. The problem of ego identity. *J. Amer. Psa. Assoc.*, 4:56–121 (1956).

32. Fisher, C. Amnesic states in war neuroses: the psychogenesis of fugues. *Psa. Quart.*, 14:437–468 (1945).

33. Fisher, C. The psychogenesis of fugue states. *Amer. J. Psychotherapy*, 1:211–220 (1947).

34. Fisher, C., and E. Joseph. Fugue with awareness of loss of personal identity. *Psa. Quart.*, 18:480–493 (1949).

35. Fisher, C. Dreams and perception: the role of preconscious and primary modes of perception in dream formation. *J. Amer. Psa. Assoc.*, 2:389–445 (1954).

36. Fisher, C. Dreams, images and perception. *J. Amer. Psa. Assoc.*, 4:5–48 (1956).

37. Freud, A. *The Ego and the Mechanisms of Defence*. New York: International Univ. Press (1946).

38. Freud, S. (1900). "The interpretation of dreams." In *The Basic Writings*. New York: Modern Library (1938), pp. 179–548.

39. Freud, S. (1904). "Psychopathology of everyday life." In *The Basic Writings*. New York: Modern Library (1938), pp. 33–178.

40. Freud, S. (1909). "Notes upon a case of obsessional neurosis." In *Collected Papers*, vol. III. London: Hogarth (1946), pp. 293–383.

41. Freud, S. (1911). "Formulations regarding the two principles in mental functioning." In *Collected Papers*, vol. IV. London: Hogarth (1946), pp. 13–21.

42. Freud, S. (1912). "Totem and taboo." In *The Basic Writings*. New York: Modern Library (1938), pp. 807–883.

43. Freud, S. (1914). "On narcissism: an introduction." In *Collected Papers*, vol. IV. London: Hogarth (1946), pp. 30–59.

44. Freud, S. (1915). "Repression." In *Collected Papers*, vol. IV. London: Hogarth (1946), pp. 84–97.

45. Freud, S. (1915). "The unconscious." In *Collected Papers*, vol. IV. London: Hogarth (1946), pp. 98–136.

46. Freud, S. (1917). "Metapsychological supplement to the theory of dreams." In *Collected Papers*, vol. IV. London: Hogarth (1946), pp. 137–151.

47. Freud, S. (1917). "Mourning and melancholia." In *Collected Papers*, vol. IV. London: Hogarth (1946), pp. 152–170.

48. Freud, S. (1923). *The Ego and the Id.* London: Hogarth (1947).
49. Freud, S. (1926). *The Problem of Anxiety.* New York: Psychoanalytic Quarterly Press (1936).
50. Froeschels, E. A peculiar intermediary state between waking and sleeping. *Amer. J. Psychotherapy,* 3:19–25 (1949).
51. Geleerd, E., F. Hacker, and D. Rapaport. Contribution to the study of amnesia and allied conditions. *Psa. Quart.,* 14:199–220 (1945).
52. Gibson, J. A critical review of the concept of set in contemporary experimental psychology. *Psychol. Bull.,* 38:781–817 (1941).
53. Gill, M., and D. Rapaport. A case of loss of personal identity and its bearing on the theory of memory. *Character and Pers.,* 11: 166–172 (1942).
54. Goldstein, K. "Methodological approach to the study of schizophrenic thought disorder." In (65), pp. 17–40.
55. Gonseth, F. *Les Fondements des mathématiques.* Paris: Librairie Scientifique Albert Blanchard (1926).
56. Hanawalt, N. Recurrent images: new instances and a summary of the older ones. *Amer. J. Psychol.,* 67:170–174 (1954).
57. Hartmann, H. Ich-Psychologie und Anpassungsproblem. *Int. Z. Psa. Imago,* 24:62–135 (1939). Abridged translation, "Ego psychology and the problem of adaptation," in (88), pp. 362–396.
58. Hebb, D. O. *The Organization of Behavior.* New York: Wiley (1949).
59. Heider, F. Die Leistung des Wahrnehmungssystems. *Z. Psychol.,* 114:371–394 (1930). Also Ding und Medium. *Symposion,* 1: 109–158 (1926).
60. Helson, H. *Theoretical Foundations of Psychology.* New York: Nostrand (1953).
61. Henderson, D., and R. Gillespie. *A Textbook of Psychiatry.* London: Oxford Univ. Press (1927).
62. Holzman, P. The relation of assimilation tendencies in visual, auditory, and kinesthetic time-error to cognitive attitudes of leveling and sharpening. *J. Pers.,* 22:375–394 (1954).
63. Isakower, O. A contribution to the pathopsychology of phenomena associated with falling asleep. *Int. J. Psa.,* 19:331–345 (1938).
64. Janet, P. *The Mental State of Hystericals.* New York: Putnam (1901).
65. Kasanin, J. S. (ed.) *Language and Thought in Schizophrenia.* Berkeley: Univ. of Calif. Press (1944).
66. Klein, G. Adaptive properties of sensory functioning: some postulates and hypotheses. *Bull. Menninger Clin.,* 13:16–23 (1949).
67. Klein, G. "Need and regulation." In M. R. Jones (ed.), *Nebraska Symposium on Motivation.* Lincoln: Univ. of Neb. Press (1954), pp. 224–274.

68. Klein, G., and H. Schlesinger. Perceptual attitudes toward instability: I. Prediction of apparent movement experiences from Rorschach responses. *J. Pers.*, 19:289–302 (1951).

69. Klein, G., and H. Schlesinger. Where is the perceiver in perceptual theory? *J. Pers.*, 18:32–37 (1949).

70. Koffka, K. *Principles of Gestalt Psychology.* New York: Harcourt, Brace (1935).

71. Kris, E. On preconscious mental processes. *Psa. Quart.*, 19:540–560 (1950). Also (abridged) in (88), pp. 474–493.

72. Kris, E. *Psychoanalytic Explorations in Art.* New York: International Univ. Press (1952).

73. Levy-Bruehl, L. *Primitive Mentality.* London: Allen and Unwin (1923).

74. Lewin, K. *A Dynamic Theory of Personality.* New York: McGraw-Hill (1935).

75. Meinong, A. Ueber Annahmen. *Z. Psychol.*, suppl. vol. II. Leipzig: Barth (1902).

76. Murphy, G. *Personality: A Biosocial Approach to Origins and Structure.* New York: Harper (1947).

77. Nachmansohn, M. "Concerning experimentally produced dreams." In (88), pp. 257–287.

78. Oldfield, R., and O. Zangwill. Head's concept of the schema and its application in contemporary British psychology, Part III. Bartlett's theory of memory. *Brit. J. Psychol.*, 33:113–129 (1942).

79. Piaget, J. *The Child's Conception of Physical Causality.* London: Kegan (1930).

80. Piaget, J. *The Child's Conception of the World.* New York: Harcourt, Brace (1929).

81. Piaget, J. "Children's philosophies." In Carl Murchison (ed.), *A Handbook of Child Psychology.* Worcester: Clark Univ. Press (1931), pp. 377–391.

82. Piaget, J. *Introduction à l'épistemologie génétique,* vols. I, II, and III. Paris: Presses Universitaires de France (1950).

83. Poetzl, O. Experimentell erregte Traumbilder in ihren Beziehungen zum indirekten Sehen. *Z. Neurol. Psychiat.*, 37:278–349 (1917).

84. Rapaport, D. The conceptual model of psychoanalysis. *J. Pers.*, 20: 56–81 (1951). Also in D. Krech and G. Klein (eds.), *Theoretical Models and Personality Theory.* Durham: Duke Univ. Press (1952), pp. 56–81. Also in R. P. Knight and C. Friedman (eds.), *Psychoanalytic Psychiatry and Psychology, Clinical and Theoretical Papers,* Austen Riggs Center, vol. I. New York: International Univ. Press (1954), pp. 221–247.

85. Rapaport, D. "Consciousness: a Psychopathological and Psychodynamic View." In *Problems of Consciousness*, Transactions of the Second Conference, March 19–20. New York: Josiah Macy, Jr., Foundation (1951), pp. 18–57.

86. Rapaport, D. *Emotions and Memory*. Baltimore: Williams and Wilkins, 1942. Second unaltered ed. New York: International Univ. Press (1950).

87. Rapaport, D. On the psycho-analytic theory of thinking. *Int. J. Psa.*, 31:161–170 (1950). Also in R. P. Knight and C. Friedman (eds.), *Psychoanalytic Psychiatry and Psychology, Clinical and Theoretical Papers*, Austen Riggs Center, vol. I. New York: International Univ. Press (1954), pp. 259–273.

88. Rapaport, D. (ed.) *Organization and Pathology of Thought*. New York: Columbia Univ. Press (1951).

89. Rapaport, D. Projective techniques and the theory of thinking. *J. Proj. Tech.*, 16:269–275 (1952). Also in R. P. Knight and C. Friedman (eds.), *Psychoanalytic Psychiatry and Psychology, Clinical and Theoretical Papers*, Austen Riggs Center, vol. I. New York: International Univ. Press (1954), pp. 196–203.

90. Rapaport, D. Review: O. Hobart Mowrer, *Learning Theory and Personality Dynamics*. *J. Abn. Soc. Psychol.*, 47:137–142 (1952).

91. Rapaport, D. Review: John Dollard and Neal E. Miller, *Personality and Psychotherapy, an Analysis in Terms of Learning, Thinking, and Culture*. *Amer. J. Orthopsychiat.*, 23:204–208 (1953).

92. Rapaport, D. Paul Schilder's contribution to the theory of thought-processes. *Int. J. Psa.*, 32:291–301 (1951).

93. Rapaport, D., R. Schafer, and M. Gill. *Diagnostic Psychological Testing*, vols. I and II. Chicago: Year Book Publishers (1945–1946).

94. Rapaport, D., and M. Erickson. Multiple personality, paper given at the meeting of the American Psychiatric Association, 1942.

95. Roffenstein, G. "Experiments on symbolization in dreams." In (88), pp. 249–256.

96. Schafer, R. *Psychoanalytic Interpretation in Rorschach Testing*. New York: Grune and Stratton (1954).

97. Schafer, R. A study of thought processes in a word association test. *Character and Pers.*, 13:212–227 (1945).

98. Scheerer, M. Problems of performance analysis in the study of personality. *Ann. N. Y. Acad. Sci.*, 46:653–675 (1946).

99. Schilder, P. *The Image and Appearance of the Human Body*. London: Kegan (1935).

100. Schilder, P. "On the development of thoughts." In (88), pp. 497–518.

101. Schilder, P. "Studies concerning the psychology and symptomatology of general paresis." In (88), pp. 519–580.

102. Schilder, P. *Medical Psychology*. New York: International Univ. Press (1953).
103. Schroetter, K. "Experimental dreams." In (88), pp. 234–248.
104. Silberer, H. "On symbol-formation." In (88), pp. 208–233.
105. Silberer, H. "Report on a method of eliciting and observing certain symbolic hallucination-phenomena." In (88), pp. 195–207.
106. Spielrein, S. Die Zeit im unterschwelligen Sellenleben. *Imago*, 9:300–317 (1923).
107. Stengel, E. On the aetiology of the fugue states. *J. Ment. Sci.*, 87: 572–599 (1941).
108. Titchener, E. *Lectures on the Experimental Psychology of the Thought Processes*. New York: Macmillan (1909).
109. Varendonck, J. *The Psychology of Daydreams*. New York: Macmillan (1921). Abridged in (88), pp. 451–473.
110. Werner, H. *Comparative Psychology of Mental Development*. New York: Harper (1940).
111. Woodworth, R. *Experimental Psychology*. New York: Henry Holt (1938).

TRENDS IN COGNITIVE THEORY

Fritz Heider

University of Kansas

THE table of contents shows that this symposium is intended to deal with the questions of whence, what, and whither. The first question — whence? — concerns the history of the problem of cognition; the second — what? — refers to some present orientations toward the problem; and the third — whither? — is asked in order to stimulate some considerations about its possible future fate.

Brunswik, in the first paper in the book, has dealt with some parts of the question "whence." However, he restricted himself more or less to perception and, one might add, to the perception of objects. Maybe you will allow me to sketch briefly a general historical frame into which one might place these cognition problems of today. I would like to start with the matrix from which scientific psychology stems: that is, with the psychology that is the basis of our actions toward other people and of our understanding them in daily life. This common-sense psychology is really not such a tender-minded psychology as many people seem to believe; it is in many respects very tough-minded. In regard to cognitive processes, it does not ask what people feel when they say "I know something." It asks, "What are the conditions that bring it about that a person knows something, and what are the effects of this knowing?" An assessment of these conditions and effects guides us in our social actions. Much of common behavior deals with cognition. Common-sense psychology is unashamedly and blatantly a cognitive psychology. I suppose we could not get on with any other psychology in dealing with other people; we have to take into account the conditions and effects of such phenomena as "keeping a secret," "telling another person something," or "showing off"; and all these phenomena imply assumptions about their cognitions.

Common-sense psychology tells us that another person can get to know about a state of affairs by directly perceiving it; he can get to know about it through inference or any kind of more rational procedure; or he can get to know about it because he gets the necessary information from another person or from reading a book or newspaper. These are a few of the conditions that we assume lead to his knowing, and this assumption we use continually in our actions referring to cognitions in other people. Common-sense psychology has also very definite assumptions about the possible effects of cognitions. One of them is an ability factor; one might call it power. If somebody knows the way to a restaurant, he will be able to get to it quickly without searching. What a person knows determines to a certain extent what he can do and what he cannot do. Another effect has to do with motivation; if I get to know that my friend is in trouble, I will be motivated to help him. If a person finds out that another person has done something that harms him, he will be motivated to take countermeasures. Cognition can also affect sentiments. When we find out something about other people, for instance about their actions, we are likely to judge them; our sentiments toward them will be changed in a favorable or unfavorable direction.

In some way we are constantly aware of all these possible conditions and effects, and we are often even aware which further factors determine the specific condition that will produce a certain one of these possible effects. All this is part of the belief-value matrix on which our actions are based. If we want to produce one of these effects in another person, then we will try to bring about one of the necessary conditions. For instance, if we want to enable another person to find the railroad station, we will tell him or we will show him the way. If we want to produce a certain motivational tendency in another person, we may tell him about a relevant situation or we may manage it so that he perceives this situation. In other cases, we may want to prevent one of these effects, and then we shall be careful to cut off the possible sources of information. These are some of the common-sense ideas about cognition, about how to deal with what another person knows and does not know.

Let us leave now this common-sense psychology and remind ourselves briefly of the fate of cognition during the development of psychology as a science. In the early days cognition played a big role. The "mind" occupied the center of the stage; it was the vessel that contained the representation of the environment. It was either considered as being furnished through the senses from the outside or as having itself fashioned its own furniture. Elementaristic and antielementaristic tendencies developed. With the rise of behaviorism, and the "glorification of the skin," we find a decline of the status of cognition. Input and output become the foci, and especially the proximal input and output, the proximal stimuli that impinge directly on the organism and on muscle contractions. I think everybody appreciates the purifying effect on psychology of this tendency. Methodologically this trend has its great value, and we have learned a lot from experiments done in this spirit. I have great sympathy with this insistence on sticking closely to what can be observed directly, and I wish it would work — it would make our task easier, though less interesting. The only trouble is that it does not work. There are too many facts that force us to change the focus.

Recently, interest has been revived in problems related to cognition. One sign is this symposium on cognition; I think somebody said that this is the first symposium on cognition. What are the reasons for this change? One cannot quite say that the facts compel people to recognize the role of cognition, because the facts have been around for a long time. They have stared psychologists in the face, but the psychologists were not aware that they were being stared at. It is more than facts, and we might think here of what Bruner said about the encoding system having to be prepared before the facts could become effective. There is, for instance, the revival of interest in perception, and one source of this revival was the role that projective tests play in clinical psychology. In social psychology, there are many phenomena that tend to make psychologists again more aware of cognitive problems. And there is one further happy accident — namely, the coming on the scene of information theory, a sort of relative of these cognitive processes which many people looked down upon and thought not quite acceptable. This relative suddenly achieved high status through being clothed in a magnificent mathematical theory, which goes far beyond anything we are used to in psychology, except, perhaps, in sense physiology, which, after all, is only of peripheral relevance to psychology. Now it is still not clear how much information theory has to do with cognitive processes, since it does not concern itself with meanings. However, one can learn a great deal from information theory. It is concerned with some kind of coordination of manifolds, and some such process is involved in cognition.

Now let us look back at the papers collected in this book. I hope you don't expect me to make a sort of dictionary of terms, a dictionary that would tell us how to translate, for instance, Bruner's concepts into those Osgood used. This would be a formidable task and I am not up to it. All I can do is to indicate a few main motifs that were taken up again and again during these sessions. I will select four of these guiding theses: (1) the foci of the different approaches, (2) the concept of representation, (3) the relation of cognition to input and output, and (4) underlying structures.

1. Our first question, then, is: what were the foci of the different approaches presented? Brunswik once wrote a paper on the conceptual focus of psychological systems (2) and we can use in trying to answer this question his scheme, which has been mentioned several times at this meeting. He lines up the relevant variables in the following way: distal stimulus — proximal stimulus — intraorganismic variables — proximal reactions — distal effects of reactions.

Brunswik, in the introductory paper of this book, discussed the relationship between the distal stimuli — that is, the objects in the environment as defined geographically and physically — and the representational processes in the person. Osgood is mainly interested in the relation between input and output, between stimuli and responses, and I do not know whether he cares whether they are defined proximally or distally. He finds that he has to use mediation as an intervening concept in order to take account of all the observations and to treat them economically. Festinger, on the other hand, deals mainly with the processes between input and output; his focal concern is with the intraorganismic variables. Of course, he makes use of stimuli and responses in his experimentation, but his primary interest seems to be directed toward something going on between them. Similarly, the coding systems of Bruner have to be placed between input and output, and also the focus of Rapaport's paper lies in this middle region. It is only natural that in a symposium on cognition most speakers concern themselves with variables lying between input and output.

2. Next, we have to consider the concept of representation. In the organism there are certain processes that in some way deal with or refer to the environment (7, p. 98). Some people (for instance, Angyal, in his book, *Foundations for a Theory of Personality*) say that this reference has something to do with symbolic representation. Angyal says, ". . . the function of the so-called mental processes is essentially a semantic one. By this we mean that 'psychological contents' function as symbols and that psychological processes are operations with these symbols" (1, p. 56). Whether or not that is an adequate description, it points to the fact that with organisms there is something going on that we do not find anywhere else — the peculiar relation of reference, of one part being correlated in a special way to another part, and at the same time being separated from it. Brunswik again and again calls our attention to this correlation between the environment and its representation in the person, and he emphasizes that the processes that mediate this relation may vary while the relation stays invariant. In visual perception, for instance, we find relatively invariant coordinations between distal stimulus and cognitive content,

which bridge the variable and vicarious mediation of light waves. Whether we conceive of this relation as being representation, symbolic function, intentionality, or invariant coordination, it certainly constitutes one of the central problems of cognition.

Let us now, with this problem in mind, consider the papers that have been presented. To begin with Brunswik, his general question is: to what extent is this relation realized? How good are these correlations between objects and their representations? According to him, the prime aspect of the cognitive problem is "the over-all correspondence between a certain distal and a certain central variable so that the former could be considered successfully mapped into the latter." The path from the distal to the central variables leads across the proximal variables, the cues, and thus the "over-all achievement arc" is broken up into an ecological and an organismic portion. The ecological portion, lying in the environment, contains the relation between objects and their cues; the organismic portion contains the relation between cues and central variables. The paper that he contributed to this meeting was particularly concerned with the part played by the ecological portion in the over-all correlation, and it contained a plea for the closer study of it.

Osgood is more interested in how the representational processes are slowly built up through contacts with the environment. For Festinger, this relationship is not a problem; it is considered as given and is accepted as such. He deals with the processes and interactions between representations. Bruner, on the other hand, refers explicitly to the phenomenon of representation, and he investigates what one might call a depth factor involved in it. In some cases representations refer to more peripheral entities and peripheral relations of the environment — the special coding systems — and in other cases they are more abstract and refer to deeper layers. The more general the encoding systems are, the more they tap the underlying invariances of the environment. I think Brunswik would use in this connection the term "depth of intention," though he did not mention it in the present paper. Finally, Rapaport adds a new aspect when he reminds us of the different ways in which the same content can be represented, and when he distinguishes among "perceptual, memorial, conceptual, hallucinatory, or dream intentions."

3. Concerning the third point — namely, the relationship of these mediating processes or representations to input and output — we can say that it is the central problem of Osgood's paper. The time is past when at least some psychologists thought that all one had to do was to measure input and output and find correlations between them. To do just that would produce the best and cleanest psychology, if nature had not put in these troublesome intervening variables, which are, moreover, connected with stimulus and response in a complicated and not very rigid way. Osgood showed that we can treat the correlations between input and output in a more economical way if we assume intervening variables that are aroused by many vicariously substitutable stimuli and that also can elicit a number of responses. That, I take it, is the meaning of his concept of mediation. The concepts of mediated transfer and mediated generalization, and also the concepts referring to integration, are supposed to have the function that is usually ascribed to cognitive concepts. I do not presume to attempt to judge how far these concepts carry. I have only the feeling that they are still too closely attached to the skin, to the proximal conditions and effects; the anchor chains are still too short.

With Festinger's experiment we come to a basically different view of the relationship between input and output, on the one hand, and cognitionlike concepts, on the other hand, and therefore also to a different experimental strategy. While Osgood starts with input and output, Festinger starts with life space or cognitive structure. He develops a plausible hypothesis concerning the relations and interactions among the contents of the life space, and then he sets up his experiment in such a way that he can test this hypothesis. If the hypothesis holds, certain actions should follow in a certain situation. Actions and situation are the observables. True enough, the connections between life space and observables are "uncritically" accepted to be simple ones. It is assumed that the person perceives the situation in the way meant by the experimenter, and that the actions are determined merely by the forces aroused by the situation and not, for instance, by a tendency to fool the experimenter. The "partition between observer and object" (5, p. 28; 3, p. 6) is in this case not located at the stimulus and the response, but rather at the boundary of the life space. The relevant variables are mainly located within the life space; the independent variables are controlled by using the situation as a tool, and the dependent variables are observed by using behavior as an indicator. It is left to the ingenuity of the experimenter to select situation and recorded behavior in such a way that they fulfill their function. I think that there can be no doubt but that this strategy is a very fruitful one and may be, at this stage of the study of cognitive processes, the only possible one. The result — the confirmation of the hypothesis — shows that the price paid — that is, neglecting to analyze the relation between observables and life space — is not too high. On the other hand, one would hope that eventually the unanalyzed assumptions of this procedure will also come under rational control.

Of course, these considerations are related to the problem of operational definition, and this might be the place to point out that there has been considerable change in modern ideas about it, a change toward a more liberal interpretation. At first, extreme operationalism was fashionable, and people thought it best to stay as close as possible to the observables. Operational definition of each concept was considered best form. At present, people who have given much thought to the problem of the empirical underpinnings of theory (Carnap, Feigl, Hempel, and others) say that this is not at all necessary, and that there are in constant use by physicists many concepts that are not in this sense operationally defined. It seems to be perfectly legitimate to use a system of concepts none of which is directly connected by simple equations to observables if only one can derive from this system testable consequences. The more often such consequences are confirmed, the more seriously one can consider the concepts as being anchored in observables. London says: "Instead . . . of a continuous one-to-one correspondence, demanded by a narrow operationism, between operations and the mathematical models employed by physical theory, only critical punctate correspondences are looked or asked for" (6, p. 243; see also 4). That is how Festinger anchored his theory in observables. One might add that this new view of the connection between theory and empirical basis is of great importance for the cognition theorist. It is not necessary that each single part of the cognitive space be connected directly with an input or output. If we succeed in building a system in such a way that it accounts for the critical inputs and outputs, then the concepts, even if they are far removed from the observables, show their validity.

4. Another recurring motif is that of the underlying structures, dispositions, or codes. So far, we have discussed only cognitive representation itself; we have also to consider the question of what makes representation possible. Representation is a function not merely of the environment; there are conditions within the organism that allow for the possibility of representation and that determine which pictures, so to speak, the organism takes of a specific environment. Rapaport's paper and Bruner's paper on the coding systems dealt with that question. We may remind ourselves of the old concept of apperceptive mass; Tolman's concept of belief-value matrix might also be mentioned in this connection. It has been remarked several times that some of Piaget's basic ideas are related to this point. His concept of assimilation refers to the influence of underlying structures on the process of cognition, and so does his concept of accommodation to changes in these structures brought about through contact with the environment. The formulations of Bruner and the observations of Rapaport give us some pointers about how to proceed in this difficult area. We certainly have to keep in mind Rapaport's admonition that "a theory of cognition will have to think both in terms of cognitive processes and in terms of cognitive organizations or structures of means character or tool character."

Our hosts who organized this symposium asked me to say a few words about prospects for the future. I hope I do not disappoint you if I abstain from making prophecies. We have

seen that the participants have touched on a great many of the
central problems of cognition. One is certainly given the feeling that the psychology of cognition is in a healthy state, with
so many people working at it in different ways. The fact that
the approaches are different seems a good thing; often the
new insights come through clashes between divergent views.
As Bruner said in his paper: two divergent coding systems
that encode the same subject matter in different ways force us
to fashion a coding system at a higher level of abstraction.

BIBLIOGRAPHY

1. Angyal, A. *Foundations for a Science of Personality.* New York: The
   Commonwealth Fund (1941).
2. Brunswik, E. The conceptual focus of some psychological systems.
   J. unified Sci., 8:36–49 (1939).
3. Brunswik, E. *The Conceptual Framework of Psycholoy.* Chicago: Univ.
   of Chicago Press (1952). (*Int. Encycl. Unified Sci.,* vol. I, no. 10.)
4. Frenkel-Brunswik, E. Psychoanalysis and the unity of science. *Proc.
   Amer. Acad. Sci.,* 80, no. 4:271–350 (1954).
5. Lenzen, V. F. *Procedures of Empirical Science.* Chicago: Univ. of
   Chicago Press (1938). (*Int. Encycl. Unified Sci.,* vol. I, no. 5.)
6. London, I. D. The role of the unneutralized symbol in psychology.
   J. gener. Psychol., 40:229–245 (1949).
7. Scheerer, M. "Cognitive theory." In G. Lindzey (ed.), *Handbook of
   Social Psychology.* Cambridge, Mass.: Addison-Wesley (1954),
   pp. 91–142.